CONTENTS

rade

CHAPTER 1 • Place Value: Whole Numbers and Decimals

CHAPTER 2 • Add and Subtract Whole Numbers and Decimals

Chapter 3 • Data, Statistics, and Graphs

Chapter 4 • Multiply Whole Numbers and Decimals

Chapter 5 • Divide by 1-Digit Divisors: Whole Numbers and Decimals

CHAPTER 6 • Divide by 2-Digit Divisors: Whole Numbers and Decimals

CHAPTER 7 • Measurement

CHAPTER 8 • Geometry

CHAPTER 9 • Fraction Concepts and Number Theory

CHAPTER 12 • Perimeter, Area, and Volume

CHAPTER 13 • Ratio, Percent, and Probability

Name: ______________________________

MILLIONS

Name the place and the value of the underlined digit.

1. 346 ______________________
2. 561 ______________________
3. 703 ______________________
4. 65,398 ______________________
5. 3,547,981 ______________________
6. 2,479,063 ______________________
7. 9,756,821 ______________________
8. 5,984,655 ______________________
9. 8,488,126 ______________________
10. 4,012,955 ______________________
11. 9,652,013 ______________________
12. 1,790,984 ______________________

Complete the table.

	Standard Form	Word Name	Expanded Form
13.		four hundred fifty-eight	
14.		one thousand, twenty-three	
15.			5,000 + 600 + 8
16.			20,000 + 3,000 + 500 + 9
17.	13,003		
18.	245,600		
19.		eight hundred thousand, two	
20.			4,000,000 + 20,000 + 90
21.	8,124,703		

Name: ________________

Compare and Order Whole Numbers

Order the numbers on the number line.

1. The numbers of baseball caps sold at four different games are 1,178; 1,201; 1,172; 1,187.

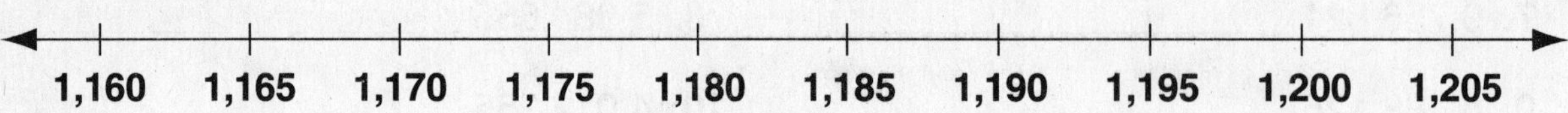

2. The numbers of people who attended four baseball games are 3,006; 2,988; 2,998; 3,016.

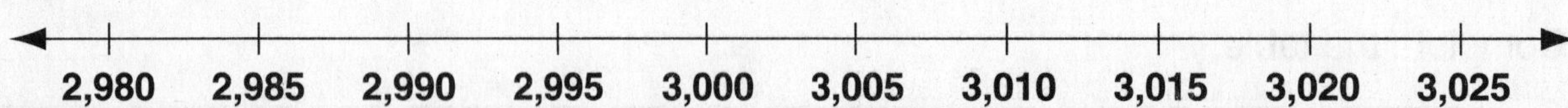

Compare. Use >, <, or =.

3. 2,976 ◯ 3,008 **4.** 8,901 ◯ 9,080 **5.** 6,698 ◯ 5,999

6. 43,032 ◯ 34,999 **7.** 98,753 ◯ 107,993 **8.** 88,901 ◯ 9,999

9. 1,645,077 ◯ 164,077 **10.** 19,463,874 ◯ 9,706,788

Order from least to greatest.

11. 190; 290; 229 ________________

12. 704; 740; 489; 699 ________________

13. 598; 1,004; 708; 2,402 ________________

14. 13,679; 13,801; 13,798 ________________

15. 7,190; 7,800; 7,660; 7,909 ________________

16. 12,660; 11,980; 12,890; 1,990 ________________

17. 28,491; 33,293; 17,301; 23,673 ________________

Name: ____________________

Problem-Solving Strategy: Make a Table

✔ Read
✔ Plan
✔ Solve
✔ Look Back

Solve using the make-a-table strategy.

1. In one orchestra, there are 8 violins for every 3 violas. If there are 32 violins in all, how many violas are there?

   ____

2. A high school has 4 singing groups, with 7 members each. Each group is made up of 2 sopranos, 1 tenor, and the rest are altos. How many of each type of singer are there?

   ____

3. The chorus teacher needs to choose songs for 3 concerts. Each concert has 14 songs. Four are solos, 3 are duets, and the rest are sung by the chorus. How many of each type of song does the teacher need to choose?

   ____

   ____

4. In a book of piano pieces, there are 4 Mozart pieces for every 2 Beethoven pieces. There are 2 Beethoven pieces for every 1 Chopin piece. If there are 3 Chopin pieces, how many Mozart pieces are there? How many Beethoven pieces?

   ____

   ____

Solve using any method.

5. In one orchestra with 100 instruments, 64 are strings. How many instruments in the orchestra are not strings?

   ____

6. In 1990, a guitar once owned by Paul McCartney was sold for $330,000. If the price had been $10,000 higher, what would the guitar have sold for?

   ____

7. **Logical Reasoning** Two orchestras have the same number of instruments. One orchestra has 42 strings and the other orchestra has 46 strings. Which one has a greater number of non-string instruments?

   ____

   ____

8. A school orchestra has 70 members. The orchestra takes 1 parent for every 10 members when it travels to another school. What is the total number of members and parents who will make each trip?

   ____

Practice 4

Name: ______________________

DECIMALS TO HUNDREDTHS

Write the decimal.

1.

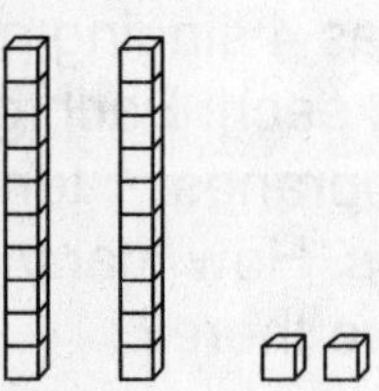

____

2.

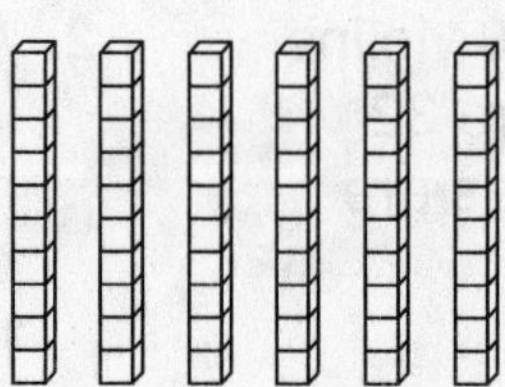

____

3.

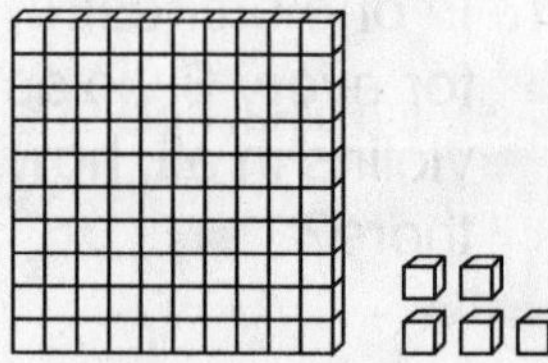

____

4.

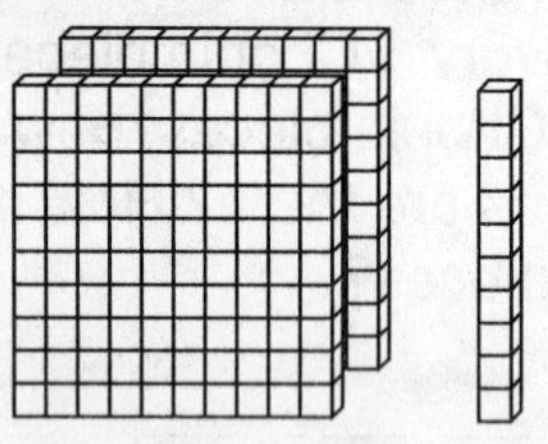

____

5.

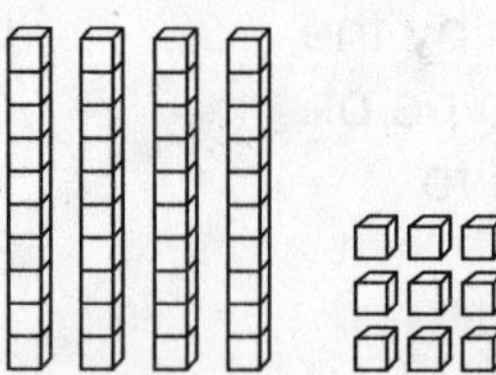

____

6.

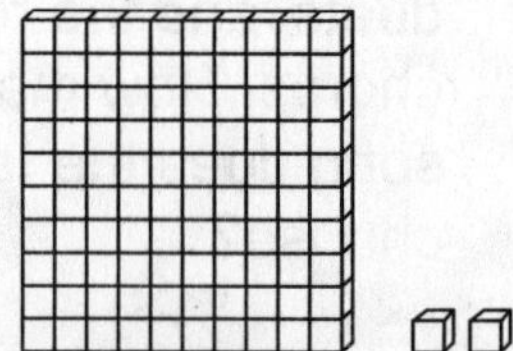

____

Name the place and the value of the underlined digit.

7. _2_.97 ______________

8. 0.8_2_ ______________

9. _5_.07 ______________

10. 15._8_3 ______________

11. 0._7_9 ______________

12. 0._6_ ______________

13. 9.9_7_ ______________

14. _2_0.90 ______________

15. 3.9_1_ ______________

16. 0._7_7 ______________

17. 4_5_.67 ______________

18. _1_8.04 ______________

Write a number:

19. 0.1 more than 3.45. ______________

20. 0.1 less than 0.7. ______________

21. 0.01 more than 0.32. ______________

22. 0.01 less than 8.75. ______________

Name: ____________________

EQUIVALENT DECIMALS

Use models to complete.

1. 2 ones = ________ tenths

2. 2 ones = ________ hundredths

3. 7 ones = ________ tenths

4. 2 tenths = ________ hundredths

5. 4 tenths = ________ hundredths

6. 6 tenths = ________ hundredths

Write the decimal and word name.

7.

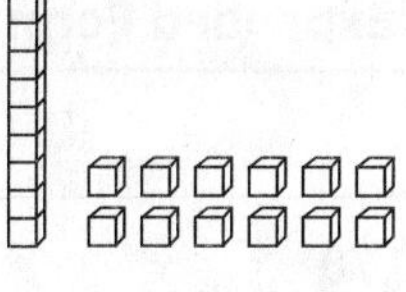

____

____

____

8.

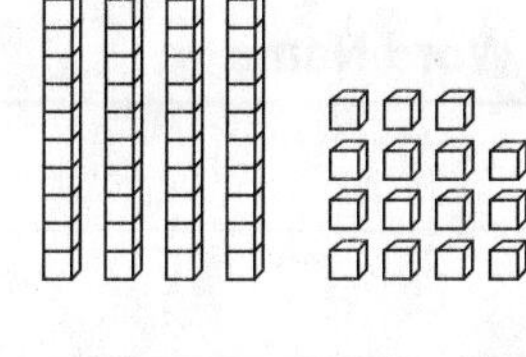

____

____

____

9.

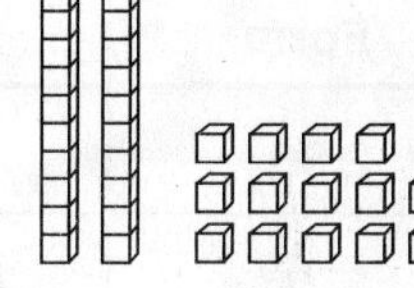

____

____

____

10.

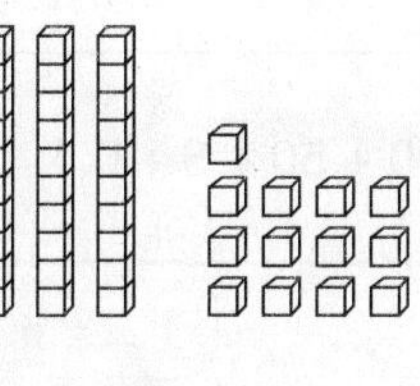

____

____

____

11.

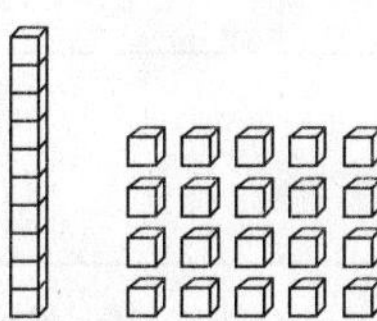

____

____

____

12.

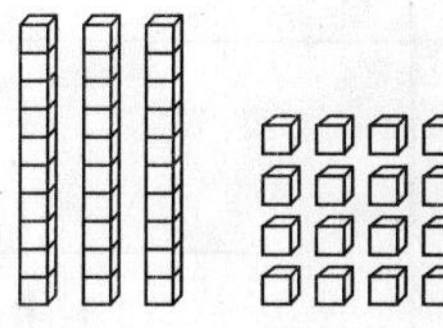

____

____

____

Name an equivalent decimal.

13. 0.2 ________

14. 0.70 ________

15. 0.6 ________

16. 16.30 ________

17. 2.6 ________

18. 4.30 ________

19. 0.40 ________

20. 1.3 ________

Name: ____________________

THOUSANDTHS

Name the place and the value of the underlined digit.

1. 2.30 ____________________ **2.** 0.18 ____________________

3. 5.078 ____________________ **4.** 26.54 ____________________

5. 9.312 ____________________ **6.** 0.892 ____________________

Complete the table.

	Standard Form	Word Name	Expanded Form
7.	2.86		
8.			5 + 0.70
9.		eight hundred sixty-three thousandths	
10.	1.12		
11.		twelve and thirty-nine thousandths	
12.	3.662		
13.			400 + 50 + 6 + 0.4
14.		thirty-three and thirty-nine hundredths	
15.	0.118		
16.	35.29		
17.			0.4 + 0.07 + 0.005
18.	193.384		

Name: ______________________

Round Whole Numbers and Decimals

Round to the place indicated.

1. 368 (tens) ______
2. 405 (hundreds) ______
3. 5,220 (thousands) ______
4. 23,102 (thousands) ______
5. 1,987 (hundreds) ______
6. 804 (tens) ______
7. 56,559 (ten thousands) ______
8. 45.6 (ones) ______
9. 12.881 (ones) ______
10. 0.82 (tenths) ______
11. 7.922 (hundredths) ______
12. 3.97 (tenths) ______
13. 1.675 (hundredths) ______
14. $56.55 (dollar) ______
15. 8.901 (ones) ______
16. 4.002 (hundredths) ______
17. $0.667 (cent) ______
18. $20.49 (dollar) ______
19. 14.432 (tenths) ______
20. 90.054 (tenths) ______
21. $123.99 (dollar) ______
22. $0.51 (dollar) ______
23. 0.993 (hundredths) ______
24. $1.399 (cent) ______
25. 2.34 (tenths) ______
26. 0.981 (tenths) ______
27. 6.098 (hundredths) ______
28. 5.356 (tenths) ______

Solve.

29. Jason read the price per gallon of three types of gasoline. They read $1.299, $1.381, and $1.496. Rounded to the nearest cent, what is the price per gallon of each type of gasoline?

______

______

30. Jason noticed that the odometer on his father's car read 74,367.5 miles. What was the mileage, to the nearest thousand miles?

______

Practice 8

Name: ____________________

Problem Solving: Interpret Bar Graphs

✔ Read
✔ Plan
✔ Solve
✔ Look Back

Use the bar graph to solve problems 1–4.

1. What was the running time in 1972? in 1992?

____

2. In what year was the fastest time run?

____

3. Would it be easier or harder to compare times if the vertical scale were marked at 2-second intervals? Explain your answer.

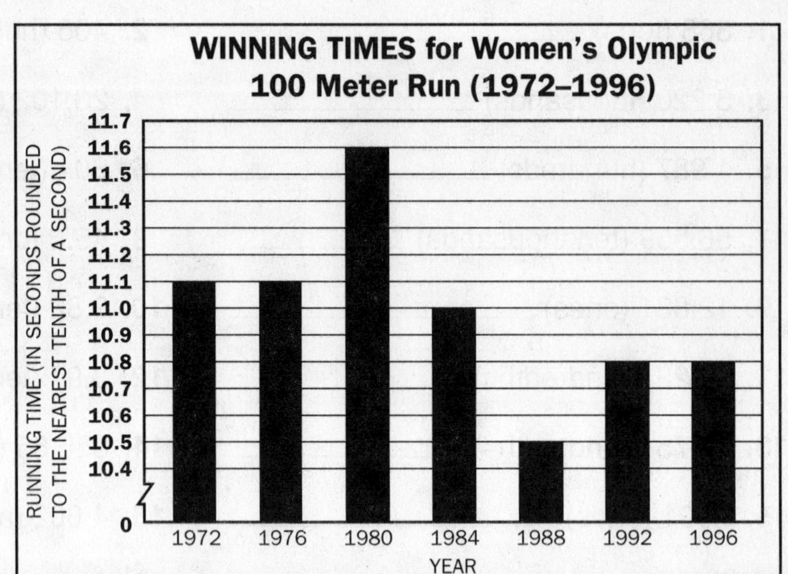

____

____

4. Write a sentence summarizing what the graph tells you.

____

____

____

Solve using any method.

5. At a school field day, Julia ran the 100-yard race in 15.46 seconds, Val in 15.39 seconds, Tanya in 14.99 seconds, and Pam in 15.07 seconds. Write the girls' names in the order in which they finished the race.

____

6. At the field day, Val ran the potato sack race in 20.362 seconds, and Pam ran it in 20.369 seconds. What place would you look at to determine who won the race?

____

Name: ____________________

Mental Math: Addition and Subtraction Strategies

Use addition properties to add mentally.

1. 7 + 9 + 3 = ______
2. $13 + $5 + $7 = ______
3. 34 + (6 + 16) = ______
4. (60 + 8) + 20 = ______
5. 14 + 11 + 56 = ______
6. 101 + 12 + 49 = ______
7. 56 + (43 + 44) = ______
8. 127 + (9 + 13) = ______

9. 67 + 34 + 6
10. 82 + 50 + 8
11. 20 + 49 + 80
12. 90 + 137 + 10
13. 92 + 53 + 8

14. 37 + 97 + 3
15. 74 + 38 + 6
16. 209 + 58 + 91
17. 194 + 12 + 88
18. 45 + 55 + 471

Use compensation to add or subtract mentally.

19. 28 + 41 = ______
20. 34 + 12 = ______
21. 249 + 97 = ______
22. 196 + 104 = ______
23. 624 − 401 = ______
24. 419 + 64 = ______
25. 568 − 29 = ______
26. 348 + 299 = ______
27. 153 − 48 = ______

Solve.

28. Brandon's lunch order totaled $2.93. He gave the cashier $10.00. How much money should he get back?

______

29. To get home from school, Brandon has to walk 6 minutes to the bus, ride the bus for 37 minutes, and then walk 4 minutes to his house. How long is his trip?

______

Name: ______

Mental Math: Estimate Sums and Differences

Estimate. Round to the nearest hundred.

1. 317 + 231 ______
2. 612 − 88 ______
3. 59 + 489 ______
4. 288 + 68 ______
5. 764 − 167 ______
6. 782 + 104 ______
7. 905 + 241 ______
8. 2,276 + 434 ______
9. $703 − $223 ______
10. 567 − 204 ______
11. 886 − 81 ______
12. 642 − 391 ______
13. 38 + 296 + 81 ______
14. 504 + 444 + 28 + 91 ______

Estimate. Round to the nearest thousand.

15. 3,425 + 8,776 ______
16. 5,319 − 1,999 ______
17. $8,553 − $2,430 ______
18. 5,609 − 3,965 ______
19. 3,498 − 743 ______
20. $6,582 − $1,421 ______
21. $2,108 − $1,071 ______
22. 9,811 − 2,339 ______
23. 12,367 + 9,145 ______
24. 14,769 − 12,299 ______
25. 12,802 + 11,210 ______
26. 14,276 + 12,922 ______
27. 4,729 + 7,246 ______
28. 924 + 642 + 1,876 ______

Solve.

29. The driving distance from Los Angeles to Chicago is 2,112 miles. The distance from Chicago to Boston is 983 miles. About how many miles is the drive from Los Angeles to Boston through Chicago?

______

30. Lisa and Kerry both live in San Francisco. Lisa's family went on vacation to Seattle, a distance of 817 miles. Kerry's family drove to Washington, D.C., a distance of 2,442 miles. About how much further did Kerry's family travel one way?

______

Name: ______________________

ADD AND SUBTRACT WHOLE NUMBERS

Find the sum or difference.

1. 347 + 561
2. $509 − 388
3. 198 + 459
4. 720 + 984
5. 467 − 293
6. $3,007 − 1,980
7. $9,868 + 6,329
8. 1,095 + 4,469
9. 3,136 − 473
10. 9,043 + 557
11. 561 + 8,410
12. 4,300 − 2,933
13. 89,441 + 98,329
14. 20,431 − 17,642
15. 31,043 + 56,631
16. 18,005 + 40,907
17. $30,048 − 19,338
18. 124,543 + 96,883
19. 321,658 − 197,369
20. 76,509 + 120,306

21. $129 + $569 + $85 = ________

22. 34,500 + 5,712 + 1,204 = ________

23. 210,336 − 89,481 = ________

24. 9,045 + 43,126 + 100,300 = ________

25. 10,557 + 21,986 + 34,018 = ________

26. 309,503 − 175,468 = ________

27. $2,980 + $135,618 = ________

28. $78,327 − $57,912 = ________

Solve.

29. The area of California is 424,002 square kilometers. New York measures 141,079 square kilometers. How many square kilometers are New York and California altogether?

____

30. The area of Texas is 695,676 square kilometers. That's 525,368 more square kilometers than Florida. What is the area of Florida in square kilometers?

____

Name: ______

PROBLEM-SOLVING STRATEGY: WRITE A NUMBER SENTENCE

✔ Read
✔ Plan
✔ Solve
✔ Look Back

Solve. Write a number sentence to show your work.

1. Mr. Andre bought prizes for his class Math Olympics. He planned to use them as gold and silver medals. For one event, one prize costs $5 and the other costs $6. If he paid with a $20 bill, how much money should he get back?

   ______

2. Students from the fourth, fifth, and sixth grades took part in the school's Math Olympics. There were 56 fourth graders, 71 fifth graders, and 68 sixth graders. How many students participated?

   ______

3. There are 85 students in the fifth grade and 78 in the sixth grade. If 95 students from those two grades participated in the school's Math Olympics, how many fifth and sixth graders did not participate?

   ______

4. Elisa and Jim participated in the paper-plane event. To qualify for the final throw, the plane must travel at least 20 feet. Elisa threw her plane 7 more feet than Jim, who threw his plane 14 feet. By how many feet did she qualify for the final throw?

   ______

Solve using any method.

5. Antonio and Raymond participated in a paper-plane event. Raymond threw a distance of 3 feet, 2 inches, and Antonio threw a distance of 2 feet, 11 inches. How much farther did Raymond throw?

   ______

6. There are 4 events in Mr. Andre's Math Olympics with 3 prizes for each event. If Mr. Andre spends about $6 on each prize, how much will he spend on all the prizes?

   ______

7. In 1896 the first modern Olympic Games were held in Athens, Greece. The seventh Olympic Games were held in Paris, France. If they are held every four years, in what year were the seventh Olympic Games held?

   ______

8. **Logical Reasoning** Four consecutive Summer Olympics were held in Spain, the United States (twice), and Korea. The Olympics in Spain were later than the one in Korea, but earlier than the second U.S. Olympics. The first U.S. Olympics was the earliest. Write the order of the four Summer Olympics.

   ______

Name: ____________________

MENTAL MATH: ESTIMATE WITH DECIMALS

Estimate.

1. 5.7 + 0.9	**2.** 13.6 − 4.7	**3.** \$1.55 + 6.08	**4.** 0.67 + 1.2
5. 6.82 − 0.36	**6.** 3.06 − 2.99	**7.** 14.71 − 8.44	**8.** 9.02 + 6.8
9. \$13.77 − 9.99	**10.** 0.82 + 8.75	**11.** 7.3 − 3.79	**12.** 90.21 + 12.45
13. 6.64 − 3.901	**14.** 0.88 + 6.336	**15.** \$1.03 + 8.50	**16.** 8.283 − 8.20
17. 44.68 − 21.555	**18.** 2.35 + 32.60	**19.** 0.86 + 3.55	**20.** 2.045 −1.56

21. 16.5 + 3.8 + 8.9 ________

22. 8.4 − 3.02 ________

23. 4.5 + 6.88 + 1.237 ________

24. 2.99 + 27.1 + 3.6 ________

25. 7.52 − 1.66 ________

26. 80.31 − 65.874 ________

27. 2.08 − 0.556 ________

28. 23.98 + 11.4 ________

29. 0.12 + 1.7 + 3.084 ________

30. \$76.08 − \$61.97 ________

Solve.

31. Jon paid for a \$2.95 sandwich and a \$1.19 drink with a \$10 bill. About how much did his lunch cost? About how much did he receive as change?

____

32. Two hiking paths begin and end at the same place. The first path is 3.89 miles long. The second path is 1.61 miles long. About how much longer is the first path than the second path?

____

Name:

ADD DECIMALS

Add. You may use place-value models.

1. 2.3 + 0.4

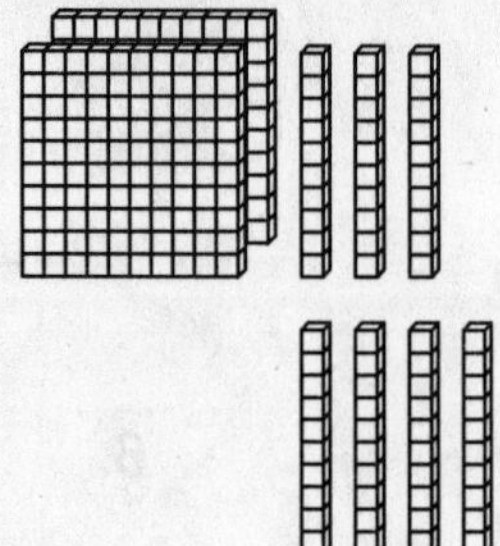

2. 1.4 + 2.3

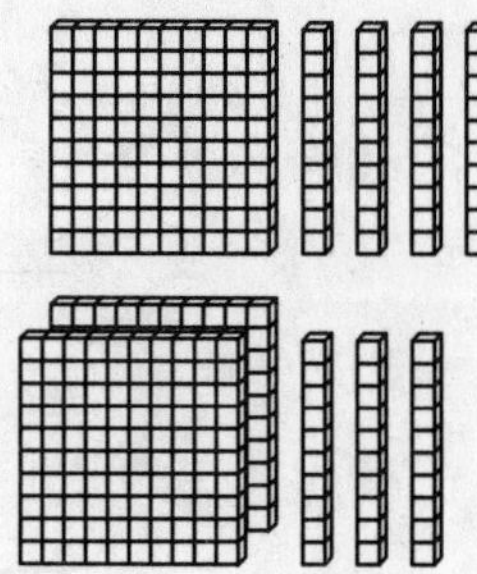

3. 1.4 + 2.5

4. 4.2 + 0.7

5. 6.7 + 3.2

6. 1.3 + 3.3

7. 1.5 + 2.2

8. 0.2 + 4.6

9. 2.6 + 0.13

10. 0.23 + 1.7

11. 0.78 + 1.6

12. 2.8 + 1.9

13. 0.54 + 0.79

14. 3.7 + 2.5

15. 4.8 + 5.8

16. 1.26 + 0.28

17. 4.12 + 2.89

18. 0.89 + 3.7

19. 3.59 + 0.7

20. 0.33 + 1.66

21. 1.98 + 2.9

22. 3.17 + 4.76

23. 3.48 + 0.77

24. 0.8 + 2.65

25. 1.90 + 3.86

26. 3.74 + 0.9

Name:

SUBTRACT DECIMALS

Subtract. You may use place-value models.

1. 1.54 − 0.43

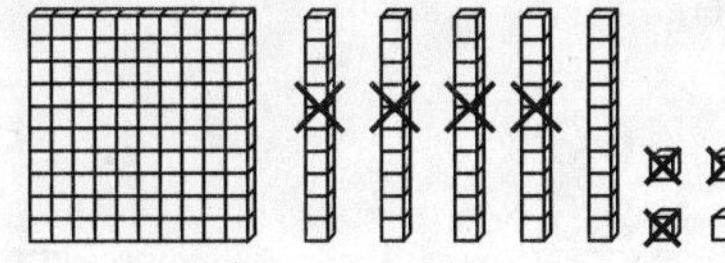

2. 2.36 − 2.22

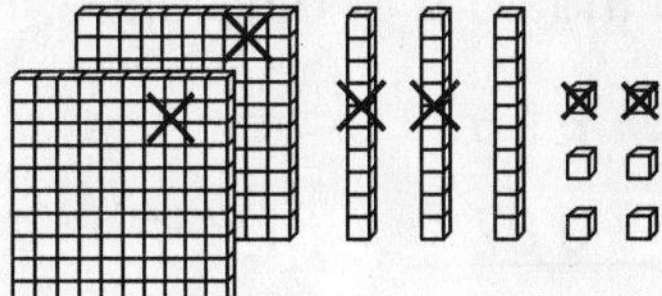

3. 3.89 − 1.23

4. 2.67 − 1.41

5. 3.78 − 2.57

6. 4.36 − 0.33

7. 1.29 − 0.18

8. 1.86 − 0.5

9. 4.92 − 2.61

10. 0.76 − 0.43

11. 2.81 − 1.39

12. 4.23 − 2.06

13. 2.94 − 0.6

14. 1.17 − 0.3

15. 3.10 − 1.2

16. 2.7 − 0.88

17. 1.66 − 0.69

18. 5.76 − 3.8

19. 3.21 − 0.44

20. 3.03 − 2.51

21. 4.51 − 1.78

22. 1.8 − 0.97

23. 4.57 − 2.98

24. 7.24 − 4.65

25. 6.21 − 4.72

26. 4.06 − 2.1

27. 3.8 − 2.73

28. 5.03 − 0.37

29. 9.97 − 9.89

30. 7.06 − 0.89

Name: ____________________

ADD AND SUBTRACT DECIMALS

Find the sum or difference. Remember to estimate.

1. 6.12 + 0.87

2. 8.87 − 0.85

3. 6.34 + 2.53

4. $3.77 − 1.44

5. 4.45 − 1.02

6. 1.55 + 7.3

7. $1.09 − 0.65

8. 0.12 − 0.04

9. 2.93 − 0.78

10. 4.809 − 2.61

11. 2.85 − 0.58

12. 6.39 + 11.21

13. 7.62 + 2.4

14. $8.02 − 6.12

15. 4.672 + 15.31

16. 7.944 − 5.33

17. 12.974 + 4.734

18. 8.294 − 3.159

19. 3.65 − 0.824

20. 5.8 + 4.289

21. 1.6 + 0.7 + 3 = ________

22. 9.54 − 4.88 = ________

23. 1.265 + 8.99 = ________

24. $44.65 − $2.19 = ________

25. 7.4 + 1.2 + 3.9 = ________

26. 0.42 + 1.234 + 6.7 = ________

27. 1.71 + 2 + 3.801 = ________

28. $55.90 − $46.72 = ________

29. 0.33 + 1.02 + 5.79 = ________

Solve.

30. Gasoline prices are given to the nearest thousandth of a cent. If gasoline rises in price from $1.599 to $1.689, what is the amount of the increase?

____

31. A race car drove 9.54 miles in one race. In another race it drove 9.82 miles. How many miles did it drive in both races?

____

Name: ______________________________

Addition and Subtraction Expressions

Evaluate the expression.

1. $a + 5$ for $a = 5$ ________
2. $m - 1$ for $m = 18$ ________
3. $p - 17$ for $p = 36$ ________
4. $92 + t$ for $t = 65$ ________
5. $145 - r$ for $r = 16$ ________
6. $x + 16.4$ for $x = 7$ ________
7. $y + 3.4$ for $y = 9$ ________
8. $6.1 - e$ for $e = 3.6$ ________
9. $65 - w$ for $w = 9.8$ ________
10. $g - 6.5$ for $g = 8.3$ ________
11. $s + 5.4$ for $s = 3.87$ ________
12. $k - 2.69$ for $k = 9.2$ ________
13. $q + 5.18$ for $q = 2.43$ ________
14. $7.12 - t$ for $t = 6.1$ ________
15. $1.8 - b$ for $b = 1.06$ ________
16. $23.6 - k$ for $k = 4.32$ ________
17. $3.16 - g$ for $g = 2.2$ ________
18. $45.3 + n$ for $n = 2.5$ ________

Complete the table.

19.

y	$6.4 + y$
3	
1.6	
4.8	

20.

m	$m - 2.1$
4.5	
5	
8.3	

21.

n	$n - 1.3$
8	
12.4	
4.2	

22.

w	$w + 0.8$
1.3	
2.9	
12.7	

23.

e	$1.8 - e$
0.8	
0.9	
1.2	

24.

x	$x - 7.6$
10	
11.2	
18.5	

Solve.

25. At the auction, someone offered $35.00 for a used bicycle. Someone else bid x dollars more. Write an expression for the amount of the greater bid. ________________

26. A set of antique books was sold for d dollars. This was $15 more than the next highest bid. Write an expression for the next highest bid. ________________

Name: ___

PROBLEM SOLVING: USE UNDERESTIMATES AND OVERESTIMATES

✔ Read
✔ Plan
✔ Solve
✔ Look Back

Solve. Write whether you used an *underestimate* or an *overestimate*.

1. Chris has some errands to run. He knows it takes him 8 minutes to walk to the cleaners, 15 minutes from the cleaners to the supermarket, 16 minutes from the supermarket to the library, and 23 minutes from the library back home. If he has to be home for dinner in 2 hours, will he have enough time to run all his errands? Explain.

2. Chris plans to spend \$7.59 at the cleaners, \$0.85 at the library, and \$6.30 at the supermarket. If he takes \$25 with him, will he have enough to pay for everything? Explain how you decided.

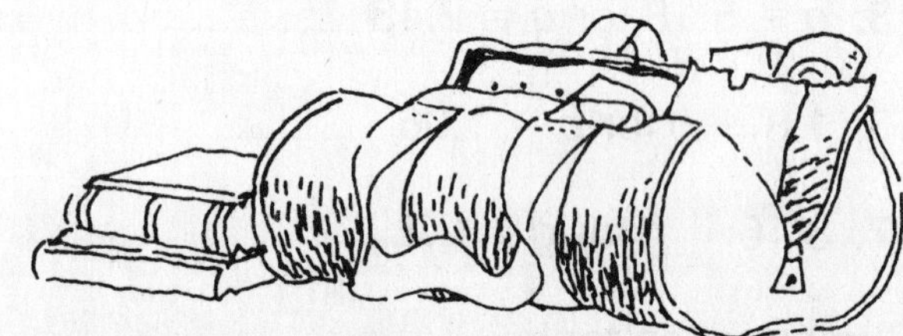

3. Chris wants to buy 2 bottles of juice for \$1.85 each and a package of candy for \$0.65. Will \$6 be enough money? Explain how you decided.

4. Chris is saving to buy his sister a sweater for \$40. He saved \$13.62 in May, \$24.19 in June, and \$10.57 in July. Has he saved enough?

Solve using any method.

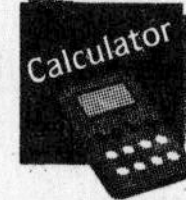

5. A neighborhood block party is being planned. The organizers want to buy 5 hot dogs for every 8 people. Complete the table to see how many hot dogs they should buy for 72 people.

People	8	16	32	64	72
Hot Dogs	5	10			

6. Jon tries a dart game at the party. The target has 3 sections—1 point, 3 points, and 5 points. If he throws 4 darts and scores 12 points, where could the darts have landed?

Name: ______________________

COLLECT, ORGANIZE, AND DISPLAY DATA

Use the line plot for problems 1–4.

Number of Blocks Students Live from School

1	2	3	4	5
		×		
		×		
		×		
	×	×		
	×	×	×	×
	×	×	×	×
×	×	×	×	×

Number of Blocks

1. How many students were surveyed?

____

2. How many students live 2 blocks from school?

____

3. How many students live the furthest distance from school?

____

4. What can you conclude from the line plot?

____

____

Use the pictograph for problems 5–7.

Servings of Fruits and Vegetables Students Ate in One Day	
Rebecca	
Charles	
Ray	
Jesse	
Corey	

Key: = 1 serving

5. How many servings of fruits and vegetables did Rebecca have? Jesse?

____

6. How many more servings did Corey have than Ray?

____

7. How would the pictograph change if each carrot stood for 2 servings?

____

Name: ______________________________

RANGE, MODE, AND MEDIAN

Find the range, median, and mode.

1. 1, 2, 5, 4, 8, 2, 2 ____________
2. 9, 4, 7, 9, 3, 10, 8 ____________
3. 3, 9, 4, 8, 5, 2, 1, 6, 3, 7 ____________
4. 5, 8, 12, 14, 10, 16 ____________
5. 12, 15, 21, 17, 32 ____________
6. 27, 31, 76, 59, 33 ____________
7. 67, 67, 98, 45, 98, 47, 89 ____________
8. 12, 20, 30, 20, 34, 49, 40, 50 ____________
9. 105, 26, 90, 50, 75, 62, 92, 78 ____________
10. $1.50, $1.50, $4.00, $5.00 ____________
11. $3.35, $6.50, $3.35, $4.35, $8.25 ____________
12. 135, 150, 135, 107, 192, 128 ____________

13.

Period	1st	2nd	3rd	4th
Points Scored	29	27	31	34

____

14.

Marking Period	1st	2nd	3rd	4th
Grade	85	90	88	87

____

15.

Day	1	2	3	4
Miles Driven	90	275	275	175

____

16.

Theater	A	B	C	D
Cost	$3.50	$4.00	$4.00	$3.50

____

Solve.

17. There are 7 baseball teams with 15, 18, 12, 13, 10, 13, and 14 players on them. What is the range, median, and mode for this data?

____

18. There are 8 clubs in a school with 9, 25, 42, 13, 28, 18, 6, and 11 students in them. What is the range, median, and mode for this data?

____

Name:

Bar Graphs

Use the single-bar graph for problems 1–4.

1. About how many students own dogs?

2. About how many more students own cats than own birds?

3. About how many students own pets that are neither cats nor dogs?

4. About how many students in the fifth grade own pets?

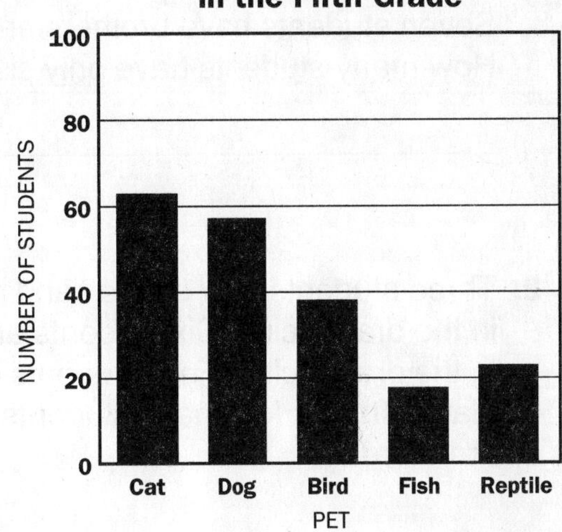

Use the double-bar graph for problems 5–8.

5. Which grade bought more lunches?

6. About how many more fifth graders than fourth graders bought lunch on Wednesday?

7. On which days did the fourth graders buy more lunches?

8. If there are 102 students in the fifth grade, how many students did not buy lunch on Monday?

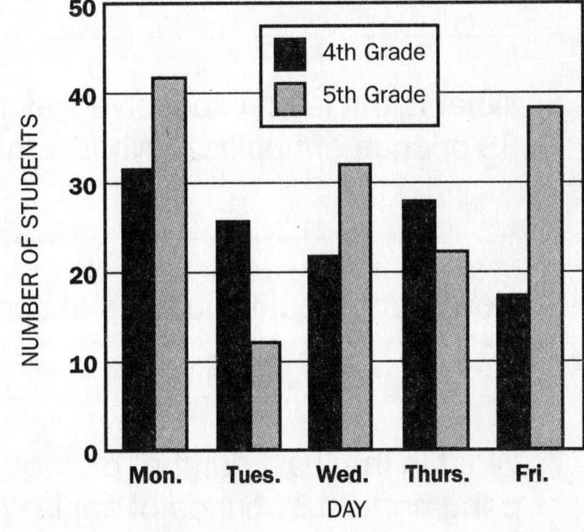

Name: ______________________________

PROBLEM-SOLVING STRATEGY: DRAW A PICTURE/DIAGRAM

✓ Read
✓ Plan
✓ Solve
✓ Look Back

Solve using the draw-a-picture/diagram strategy.

1. There are 27 students in the class with siblings. Eleven students have brothers. Seven students have brothers and sisters. How many students have only sisters?

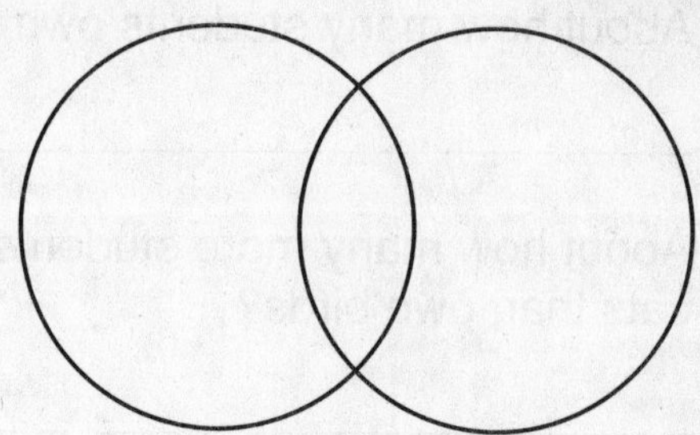

____

2. Three students play softball and are in the drama club. Six students are just in the drama club. Four students only play softball. How many students are there?

____

3. There are 35 students. At lunch, 3 students ate only apples, and 9 students ate only oranges. 18 students ate both apples and oranges. How many students ate neither?

____

Solve using any method.

4. Apples can only be bought in the sizes shown. What is the least expensive way to buy 13 pounds of apples? What is the cost?

____

5. What is the least expensive way to buy 35 pounds of apples? What is the cost?

____

6. How much would you have to spend for 9 pounds of apples?

____

7. What is the least number of bags you must carry in order to bring home 18 pounds of apples?

____

Name:

LINE GRAPHS

Use the line graph for problems 1–4.

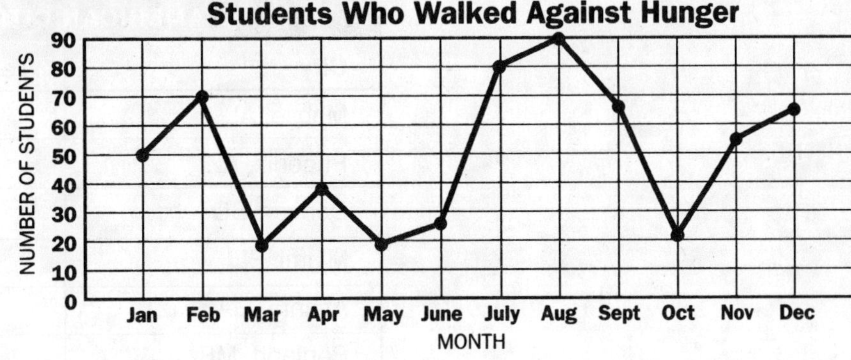

1. How many students walked against hunger in December?

2. In what month did the greatest number of students walk against hunger?

3. In what months did an equal number of students walk against hunger?

4. Between which months was there the greatest decrease in the number of students?

Use the table for problems 5–9.

5. Use the information in the table to make a line graph.

6. During which two-hour period was there the greatest number of people in the bank?

7. During which two-hour period was there the least number of people in the bank?

8. Between which two hours was there the greatest decrease in the number of people in the bank?

NUMBER OF PEOPLE IN A BANK	
Time	**Number of People**
8 A.M.	8
9 A.M.	6
10 A.M.	5
11 A.M.	10
12 noon	12
1 P.M.	4
2 P.M.	8
3 P.M.	5
4 P.M.	7
5 P.M.	8

Name: ______________________________

Stem-and-Leaf Plots

Make a stem-and-leaf plot for the data.

AVERAGE JANUARY TEMPERATURES IN SOME AMERICAN CITIES IN °F	
City	**Temperature**
Mobile, AL	53°
Phoenix, AZ	54°
Denver, CO	33°
Miami, FL	68°
Atlanta, GA	43°
Portland, ME	23°
Reno, NV	35°
Buffalo, NY	25°
Houston, TX	53°
Richmond, VA	38°
Des Moines, IA	22°

Use the stem-and-leaf plot and chart for problems 1–6.

1. How many cities have average temperatures above 50°F?

   ____

2. Which two cities have the highest average temperatures?

   ____

3. Find the range, median, and mode for the data.

   ____

4. Which two cities have the lowest average temperatures?

   ____

5. What conclusion can you draw from the stem-and-leaf plot?

   ____

6. What if 2 additional cities had average temperatures between 40°F and 50°F? How would the stem-and-leaf plot change?

   ____

Name:

Problem Solving: Choose the Appropriate Graph

✔ Read
✔ Plan
✔ Solve
✔ Look Back

Solve.

1. The fifth grade has a fundraiser. The first week they collect $59, the second $81, the third $60, and the fourth $65. What type of graph would best display this data? Why?

2. For a fundraiser 16 students sold raffle tickets, 19 students sold chocolate bars, and 10 students sold candied apples. What type of graph would best display this data? Why?

3. What type of graph would best display the following data? Why?

AMOUNT OF MONEY EARNED EACH WEEK				
	1	2	3	4
raffle	$36	$32	$25	$43
candy	$23	$49	$35	$22

4. The students who sold the most chocolate bars were Jim, who sold 85, Alex, who sold 65, Nancy, who sold 120, and Max, who sold 105. What type of graph would best display this data? Why?

Solve using any method.

5. In the snack bar 27 people bought just pretzels. Fourteen bought a soft drink and a pretzel. Twelve just bought soft drinks. How many pretzels and soft drinks were sold?

6. Fifteen friends went to a bowling party. Four rented size 6 shoes. Six rented size 7 shoes. The rest rented size 5 shoes. How many pairs of size 5 shoes were rented?

Name: ________________________________

Mental Math: Use Multiplication Patterns

Use mental math to complete the pattern.

1. $5 \times 1 = 5$
$5 \times 10 = 50$
$5 \times 100 =$ ________
$5 \times 1{,}000 =$ ________

2. $8 \times 2 = 16$
$8 \times 20 = 160$
$8 \times 200 =$ ________
$8 \times 2{,}000 =$ ________

3. $2 \times 50 = 100$
$20 \times 50 = 1{,}000$
$200 \times 50 =$ ________
$2{,}000 \times 50 =$ ________

4. $9 \times 1 = 9$
$9 \times 10 = 90$
$9 \times 100 =$ ________
$9 \times 1{,}000 =$ ________

5. $3 \times 6 = 18$
$3 \times 60 = 180$
$3 \times 600 =$ ________
$3 \times 6{,}000 =$ ________

6. $7 \times 30 = 210$
$70 \times 30 = 2{,}100$
$700 \times 30 =$ ________
$7{,}000 \times 30 =$ ________

7. $1 \times \$1.86 = \$1.86$
$10 \times \$1.86 = \$18.60$
$100 \times \$1.86 =$ ________
$1{,}000 \times \$1.86 =$ ________

8. $1 \times 7.93 = 7.93$
$10 \times 7.93 = 79.3$
$100 \times 7.93 =$ ________
$1{,}000 \times 7.93 =$ ________

9. $1 \times 2.061 = 2.061$
$10 \times 2.061 = 20.61$
$100 \times 2.061 =$ ________
$1{,}000 \times 2.061 =$ ________

Multiply mentally.

10. $6 \times 50 =$ ________
11. $90 \times 3 =$ ________
12. $400 \times 7 =$ ________
13. $2 \times 3{,}000 =$ ________
14. $60 \times 80 =$ ________
15. $800 \times 40 =$ ________
16. $200 \times 50 =$ ________
17. $700 \times 60 =$ ________
18. $80 \times 3{,}000 =$ ________
19. $10 \times 5.9 =$ ________
20. $0.021 \times 100 =$ ________
21. $10 \times 0.8 =$ ________
22. $100 \times \$8.93 =$ ________
23. $\$2.06 \times 10 =$ ________
24. $10 \times 2.985 =$ ________

Solve.

25. Anthony pays $1.25 to ride the bus to school each day. How much will he pay for 100 trips?

____

26. Ramona buys 7 packs of paper with 50 sheets in each pack. How many sheets of paper does she have in all?

____

Name: ____________________

Mental Math: Estimate Products

Estimate the product by rounding.

1. 3 × 127 ________
2. 7 × 889 ________
3. 5 × 1,123 ________
4. 96 × 83 ________
5. 24 × 47 ________
6. 51 × 82 ________
7. 29 × 603 ________
8. 223 × 797 ________
9. 82 × 3,789 ________
10. 780 × 11.3 ________
11. 19 × 876 ________
12. 46 × 408 ________
13. 8 × $56 ________
14. 12 × $35 ________
15. 7 × 3,045 ________
16. 22 × $321 ________
17. 19 × $189.84 ________
18. 679 × 3.1 ________
19. 38 × 8.5 ________
20. 29 × 37.6 ________
21. 5.7 × 3,498 ________
22. 24 × 5.13 ________
23. 38 × 14.1 ________
24. 67 × 6.42 ________
25. 61 × $509 ________
26. 13 × $2.32 ________
27. 25 × 92 ________
28. 91 × 3.2 ________
29. 21 × 5.2 ________
30. 426 × 13.4 ________

Estimate. Write <, >, or =.

31. 5 × 804 ◯ 4,326
32. 3 × 6,008 ◯ 17,980
33. 6 × 439 ◯ 2,299
34. 9,000 ◯ 12 × 893
35. 32 × 633 ◯ 1,800
36. 2,096 ◯ 32 × 67
37. 95 × $87.23 ◯ $8,003
38. 32,471 ◯ 492 × 836

Solve.

39. The nutritionist is ordering food for school lunches for the next few months. She orders 346 cartons of pasta. Each carton contains 18 boxes of pasta. About how many boxes does the nutritionist order?

____

40. The nutritionist also needs to order milk. If there are 876 students, and each student drinks one container a day, about how many containers of milk does she need to order for one school week?

____

Name: ____________________

USE THE DISTRIBUTIVE PROPERTY

Complete. Write the correct sign or number.

1. 8 × 13 = 8 × (10 + ☐)

2. 4 × 21 = 4 × (☐ + 1)

3. 4 × 83 = ☐ × (80 + 3)

4. 8 × 609 = 8 × (600 ◯ 9)

5. 8 × 19 = 8 × (10 ◯ 9)

6. 3 × 68 = 3 × (☐ + 8)

7. 7 × 207 = 7 × (200 ◯ 7)

8. 5 ◯ 46 = (5 × 40) + (5 × 6)

9. 8 ◯ 76 = (8 × 70) + (8 × 6)

10. 5 × 56 = (5 × 50) ◯ (5 × 6)

11. 2 × 93 = (2 × 90) + (☐ × 3)

12. 6 × 89 = (6 × ☐) + (6 × 9)

13. 9 × (30 + 8) = (9 × 30) + (☐ × 8)

14. (20 + 9) × 5 = (20 ◯ 5) + (9 × 5)

Multiply.

15. 5 × 13 = ______

16. 4 × 76 = ______

17. 7 × 19 = ______

18. 8 × 58 = ______

19. 9 × 98 = ______

20. 4 × 97 = ______

21. 3 × 71 = ______

22. 9 × 56 = ______

23. 8 × 34 = ______

24. 2 × 27 = ______

25. 4 × 83 = ______

26. 8 × 17 = ______

27. 9 × 35 = ______

28. 5 × 65 = ______

29. 8 × 22 = ______

30. 8 × 33 = ______

31. 4 × 81 = ______

32. 5 × 94 = ______

33. 9 × 16 = ______

34. 4 × 51 = ______

35. 6 × 88 = ______

36. 4 × 77 = ______

37. 7 × 103 = ______

38. 3 × 221 = ______

39. 3 × 346 = ______

40. 2 × 906 = ______

41. 2 × 881 = ______

42. 7 × 305 = ______

43. 2 × 972 = ______

44. 3 × 198 = ______

45. 6 × 106 = ______

46. 5 × 206 = ______

47. 8 × 307 = ______

Name:

Multiply by 1-Digit Numbers

Find the product. Remember to estimate.

1. 18 × 6
2. 67 × 3
3. 43 × 2
4. 21 × 5
5. 46 × 8

6. 64 × 7
7. $92 × 7
8. 64 × 9
9. $59 × 9
10. 371 × 4

11. 507 × 7
12. 284 × 2
13. 440 × 6
14. $183 × 2
15. 503 × 6

16. 781 × 4
17 984 × 7
18. 769 × 4
19. 3,297 × 2
20. 2,904 × 3

21. 6 × 135 = ________
22. 3 × 374 = ________
23. 3 × 5,012 = ________

24. 7 × 2,436 = ________
25. 4 × 12,261 = ________
26. 6 × 10,451 = ________

Solve.

27. At a barbecue, the cook grills 2 pieces of chicken and 4 potato wedges for each guest. If 23 people attend, how many chicken pieces and potato wedges must the cook grill?

____

____

28. At the barbecue, the children have a water balloon fight. Each child has 9 balloons. If there are 13 children, how many balloons do they have?

____

____

Name: ______________________________

Problem-Solving Strategy: Solve Multistep Problems

✔ Read
✔ Plan
✔ Solve
✔ Look Back

Solve. Use the newsletter for problems 1–3.

Harrison Middle School NEWSLETTER

Once again, Harrison's fifth grade prepares for its annual "Feed the Homeless" program to collect cans of food for the needy.

This year, students and their families are being asked to contribute 4 cans. This is 1 can up from last year's requested contribution.

There is, of course, no limit as to how much you can give. So if you are willing and able to donate more, the school thanks you.

1. The fifth grade is divided into three classes of 23, 20, and 22 students. How many cans of food can the fifth-grade students collect this year if there are no extras? How many would they have collected last year if there were no extras?

____

____

2. If 17 students in the fifth grade decided they each could contribute 5 cans, and 3 students decided they each could contribute 6 cans, how many extra cans of food could be collected for the homeless this year?

____

____

3. Last year, 7 of the 65 fifth graders never received the "Feed the Homeless" newsletter. If the remaining fifth graders each contributed exactly the amount requested, how many cans were collected last year?

____

Solve using any method.

Type of Food	Soup	Vegetables	Beans
Number of Cans	113	68	182

4. Each of four volunteers delivers 8 cans of soup, 5 cans of vegetables, and 12 cans of beans. How many cans do they deliver in all?

____

5. The following amounts are the number of cans collected from each grade level.

326, 439, 219, 146, 350, 420, 350

What is the range, median, and mode for this set of data?

____

Name: ______________________________

MULTIPLY BY 2-DIGIT NUMBERS

Find the product. Remember to estimate.

1. 76 × 40
2. 97 × 30
3. 214 × 31
4. 345 × 42
5. 606 × 23

6. 189 × 52
7. 835 × 35
8. 554 × 62
9. 803 × 38
10. $568 × 20

11. $2,490 × 60
12. 6,351 × 47
13. $5,997 × 56
14. 8,812 × 52
15. $3,006 × 28

16. 12,638 × 49
17. 11,362 × 25
18. $31,999 × 13
19. 31,456 × 17
20. 30,045 × 21

21. 43 × 65 = ________
22. 90 × 22 = ________
23. 35 × $77 = ________

24. 30 × 87 = ________
25. 67 × 103 = ________
26. 14 × 409 = ________

Use estimation to determine whether the product is less than or greater than the given number. Check by finding the product.

27. 15 × 75; 2,200 ________________
28. 31 × $59; $1,653 ________________

Solve.

29. Dog food comes in 25-pound bags. The pet store ordered 575 bags. How many pounds of dog food did the store order?

____

30. Dog biscuits come in 4-pound boxes, with 12 boxes to a case. The store ordered 124 cases. How many pounds of dog biscuits did the store order?

____

Name: ____________________

Multiply Decimals by Whole Numbers

Estimate. Then place the decimal point.

1. 4 × 1.67 = 6 6 8
2. 8 × 2.74 = 2 1 9 2
3. 6 × $0.79 = $4 7 4
4. 5 × 0.8 = 4 0

Multiply. Remember to estimate to place the decimal point.

5. 0.6 × 8
6. 0.8 × 7
7. 1.4 × 3
8. 6.3 × 8
9. $0.89 × 4
10. $0.72 × 4
11. 1.44 × 2
12. $2.71 × 5
13. $34.99 × 14
14. $17.45 × 56
15. $99.05 × 49
16. $107.44 × 25
17. 28.12 × 53
18. 54.87 × 78
19. 23.42 × 94
20. 77.69 × 62

Solve.

21. Each Sunday during his 9-week summer vacation, Ray buys a newspaper for his parents. The paper costs $1.55 per week. How much does he pay for all the newspapers in 2 summers?

____

22. One Sunday Ray weighed the newspaper and found that it weighed 2.7 pounds. If each Sunday newspaper weighs the same, how many pounds of newspaper will Ray's family recycle if they buy 52 Sunday papers?

____

Name: ____________________

Use Models to Multiply

Find the product.

1. 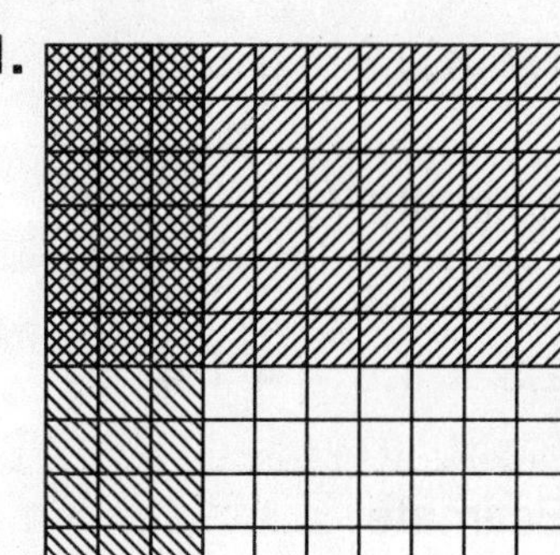
____

2. _______________

3. 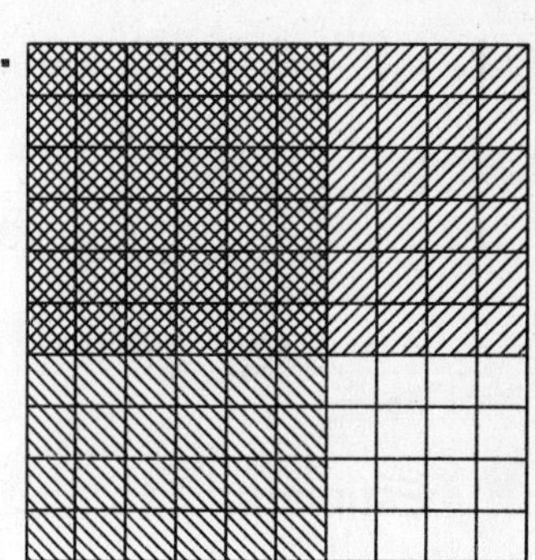
____

Find the product. You may use graph paper to help you multiply.

4. $\begin{array}{r} 0.2 \\ \times\ 0.3 \\ \hline \end{array}$

5. $\begin{array}{r} 0.5 \\ \times\ 0.5 \\ \hline \end{array}$

6. $\begin{array}{r} 0.4 \\ \times\ 0.2 \\ \hline \end{array}$

7. $\begin{array}{r} 0.3 \\ \times\ 0.6 \\ \hline \end{array}$

8. $\begin{array}{r} 0.7 \\ \times\ 0.8 \\ \hline \end{array}$

9. $\begin{array}{r} 0.6 \\ \times\ 0.7 \\ \hline \end{array}$

10. $\begin{array}{r} 0.4 \\ \times\ 0.5 \\ \hline \end{array}$

11. $\begin{array}{r} 0.5 \\ \times\ 0.9 \\ \hline \end{array}$

12. $\begin{array}{r} 0.1 \\ \times\ 0.6 \\ \hline \end{array}$

13. $\begin{array}{r} 0.4 \\ \times\ 0.9 \\ \hline \end{array}$

14. $\begin{array}{r} 0.6 \\ \times\ 0.9 \\ \hline \end{array}$

15. $\begin{array}{r} 0.8 \\ \times\ 0.8 \\ \hline \end{array}$

16. Find the product of 0.8 and 0.3. ________

17. Find the product of 0.8 and 0.9. ________

18. What is 0.4 times 0.1? ________

19. What is 0.6 times 0.8? ________

20. The factors are 0.6 and 0.5. What is the product? ________

21. The factors are 0.2 and 0.6. What is the product? ________

Name: ______________________

MULTIPLY WITH DECIMALS

Estimate. Then place the decimal point in the product.

1. 0.5 × 0.6 = 0 3 0

Estimate: ________

2. 2.6 × 1.4 = 3 6 4

Estimate: ________

3. 1.7 × 0.9 = 1 5 3

Estimate: ________

4. 4.9 × 0.8 = 3 9 2

Estimate: ________

5. 0.98 × 0.9 = 0 8 8 2

Estimate: ________

6. 2.3 × 1.8 = 4 1 4

Estimate: ________

7. 5.1 × 2.7 = 1 3 7 7

Estimate: ________

8. 6.09 × 8.6 = 5 2 3 7 4

Estimate: ________

9. 5.78 × 7.7 = 4 4 5 0 6

Estimate: ________

10. 21.7 × 8.4 = 1 8 2 2 8

Estimate: ________

11. 3.72 × 1.3 = 4 8 3 6

Estimate: ________

12. $65.2 × 3.6 = $2 3 4 7 2

Estimate: ________

Multiply. Remember to estimate to place the decimal point.

13. 0.88 × 0.6

14. 7.4 × 0.4

15. 4.35 × 0.7

16. 3.47 × 0.9

17. 5.82 × 6.8

18. 3.06 × 1.9

19. 90.2 × 2.8

20. 1.76 × 5.2

Solve.

21. One trail in a campground's park is 3.36 miles long. If you hike that trail each day for 4 days, how far will you have walked in all?

____

22. Another trail in the park is 2.57 miles long. If you hike that trail each day for 5 days, how far will you have walked in all?

____

Name:

Zeros in the Product

Multiply.

1. 0.004×5
2. 0.004×9
3. 0.002×7
4. 0.002×6
5. 0.024×2
6. 0.25×0.3
7. 0.04×1.5
8. 0.01×6
9. 0.34×3
10. 0.009×12
11. 0.014×16
12. 0.008×11
13. 0.203×31
14. 0.007×13
15. 0.005×19
16. 0.45×0.2
17. 0.16×0.2
18. 15.2×0.4
19. 18.7×0.3
20. 1.21×0.05

21. $3 \times 0.015 =$ ______
22. $4 \times 0.012 =$ ______
23. $3 \times 0.025 =$ ______
24. $3 \times 3.01 =$ ______
25. $5 \times 0.008 =$ ______
26. $0.7 \times 1.02 =$ ______

Compare. Write $>$, $<$, or $=$.

27. 0.06×0.3 ◯ 0.018
28. 2.03×0.3 ◯ 0.0609
29. 1.8×0.01 ◯ 0.18
30. 0.02×0.3 ◯ 0.2×0.03

Solve.

31. When doing his math homework, Leroy multiplies 0.035 by 0.2 and gets 0.07. What did he do wrong and what is the correct answer?

______

______

32. On another homework problem Susan multiplies 0.021 by 0.7 and gets 0.147. What did she do wrong and what is the correct answer?

______

______

Name:

Problem Solving: Make a Table

✔ Read
✔ Plan
✔ Solve
✔ Look Back

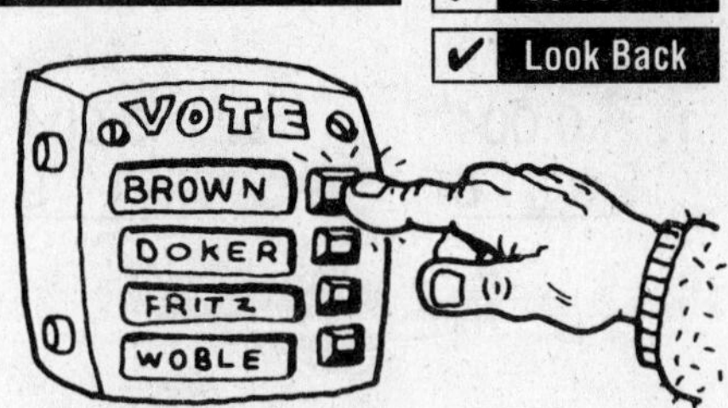

On election day, the Don't-Forget-to-Vote Committee started making phone calls to remind people to vote. The person in the office called 4 people. Then each of those people called 4 people. They did this until all the voters in town were called.

Round of Phone Calls	1	2	3	4	5	6
Number of Voters Called	4	16	64			
Total Voters Called	4	20	84			

Solve using the make-a-table strategy. Use the information above for problems 1–4.

1. Complete the table. What patterns do you see?

2. How many voters were called in the 5th round?

3. How many rounds did it take to call all the voters in town?

4. **What if** each caller made 2 calls each round. How many rounds would it take to call all the voters?

Solve using any method.

5. There are 5 different places where voters can go to vote. If 5,460 people vote, and the same number of voters goes to each of the 5 places, how many voters will go to each place?

6. There's a van provided on election day between 11 A.M. and 3:30 P.M. The van holds 12 people. It takes 45 minutes to make one complete round. If the van is full every time, how many people ride to the voting booth?

Name: Practice 37

MEANING OF DIVISION

Divide.

1. $4\overline{)12}$ 2. $5\overline{)20}$ 3. $2\overline{)16}$ 4. $6\overline{)36}$ 5. $3\overline{)27}$

6. $2\overline{)14}$ 7. $4\overline{)36}$ 8. $6\overline{)24}$ 9. $6\overline{)30}$ 10. $6\overline{)48}$

11. $3\overline{)13}$ 12. $4\overline{)9}$ 13. $5\overline{)27}$ 14. $6\overline{)20}$ 15. $5\overline{)34}$

16. $7\overline{)51}$ 17. $5\overline{)38}$ 18. $8\overline{)70}$ 19. $7\overline{)31}$ 20. $7\overline{)64}$

21. $\frac{54}{9}$ _____ 22. $\frac{45}{5}$ _____ 23. $\frac{81}{9}$ _____ 24. $\frac{72}{8}$ _____ 25. $\frac{42}{7}$ _____

26. $\frac{18}{7}$ _____ 27. $\frac{41}{5}$ _____ 28. $\frac{30}{6}$ _____ 29. $\frac{63}{9}$ _____

30. $52 \div 8$ _____ 31. $54 \div 9$ _____ 32. $48 \div 8$ _____ 33. $32 \div 7$ _____

34. $49 \div 6$ _____ 35. $19 \div 9$ _____ 36. $68 \div 7$ _____ 37. $58 \div 6$ _____

38. The dividend is 63 and the quotient is 9. What is the divisor? _____

39. The dividend is 36 and the divisor is 6. What is the quotient? _____

Solve.

40. Jasmine has 48 computer disks in 8 cases. If she divides the disks equally among the cases, how many will be in each case?

_____

41. Julie's hard drive has 63 files saved on it. She wants to divide them equally among 9 folders. How many files will go in each folder?

_____

Name: ______ **Practice 38**

MENTAL MATH: USE DIVISION PATTERNS

Use mental math to complete the pattern.

1. 16 ÷ 8 = 2
160 ÷ 8 = 20
1,600 ÷ 8 = ______

2. 45 ÷ 9 = 5
450 ÷ 9 = 50
4,500 ÷ 9 = ______

3. 63 ÷ 7 = 9
630 ÷ 7 = 90
6,300 ÷ 7 = ______

4. 42 ÷ 7 = 6
420 ÷ 7 = 60
4,200 ÷ 7 = ______

5. 56 ÷ 8 = 7
560 ÷ 8 = 70
5,600 ÷ 8 = ______

6. 30 ÷ 6 = 5
300 ÷ 6 = 50
3,000 ÷ 6 = ______

7. 24 ÷ 4 = 6
240 ÷ 4 = 60
2,400 ÷ 4 = ______
24,000 ÷ 4 = ______

8. 49 ÷ 7 = 7
490 ÷ 7 = 70
4,900 ÷ 7 = ______
49,000 ÷ 7 = ______

9. 54 ÷ 6 = 9
540 ÷ 6 = 90
5,400 ÷ 6 = ______
54,000 ÷ 6 = ______

Divide mentally.

10. $3\overline{)30}$ **11.** $2\overline{)60}$ **12.** $5\overline{)50}$ **13.** $4\overline{)80}$

14. $6\overline{)120}$ **15.** $6\overline{)360}$ **16.** $9\overline{)270}$ **17.** $7\overline{)210}$

18. $7\overline{)280}$ **19.** $5\overline{)250}$ **20.** $9\overline{)720}$ **21.** $8\overline{)640}$

22. $6\overline{)600}$ **23.** $3\overline{)900}$ **24.** $7\overline{)1{,}400}$ **25.** $2\overline{)1{,}200}$

26. 180 ÷ 3 = ____ **27.** 240 ÷ 6 = ____ **28.** 360 ÷ 9 = ____ **29.** 300 ÷ 6 = ____

30. 2,100 ÷ 3 = ______ **31.** 2,000 ÷ 4 = ______ **32.** 3,600 ÷ 4 = ______

33. 2,400 ÷ 6 = ______ **34.** 7,000 ÷ 7 = ______ **35.** 40,000 ÷ 5 = ______

36. 16,000 ÷ 4 = ______ **37.** 27,000 ÷ 9 = ______ **38.** 18,000 ÷ 3 = ______

39. 15,000 ÷ 3 = ______ **40.** 16,000 ÷ 8 = ______ **41.** 72,000 ÷ 8 = ______

Name: ______________________

Mental Math: Estimate Quotients

Estimate. Write a division sentence to show how you estimated.

1. 175 ÷ 9 ____________
2. 231 ÷ 6 ____________
3. 139 ÷ 7 ____________
4. 345 ÷ 6 ____________
5. 410 ÷ 7 ____________
6. 453 ÷ 9 ____________
7. 288 ÷ 7 ____________
8. 149 ÷ 4 ____________
9. 660 ÷ 8 ____________
10. 5,833 ÷ 8 ____________
11. 3,079 ÷ 5 ____________
12. 4,748 ÷ 7 ____________
13. 1,836 ÷ 6 ____________
14. 4,194 ÷ 8 ____________
15. 2,660 ÷ 9 ____________
16. 8,004 ÷ 9 ____________
17. 8,233 ÷ 8 ____________
18. 7,193 ÷ 8 ____________
19. 14,798 ÷ 5 ____________
20. 23,808 ÷ 4 ____________
21. 43,243 ÷ 5 ____________
22. $7\overline{)345}$ ____________
23. $6\overline{)431}$ ____________
24. $8\overline{)629}$ ____________
25. $2\overline{)155}$ ____________
26. $9\overline{)290}$ ____________
27. $7\overline{)501}$ ____________
28. $4\overline{)310}$ ____________
29. $3\overline{)1,464}$ ____________
30. $2\overline{)1,179}$ ____________

Solve using estimation.

31. Mark wanted to wrap the 235 pennies he had collected into rolls to take to the bank. He put the pennies into 5 stacks. About how many pennies were in each stack?

____

32. By collecting pennies over several years, Mark saved $123. He decided to use the money to take 3 friends to an amusement park. He spent the same amount on each friend and himself. About how much did each person get?

____

Practice 40

Name:

DIVIDE WHOLE NUMBERS

Divide mentally.

1. $6\overline{)38}$ 2. $3\overline{)99}$ 3. $8\overline{)120}$ 4. $4\overline{)164}$

5. $5\overline{)461}$ 6. $5\overline{)183}$ 7. $7\overline{)427}$ 8. $6\overline{)195}$

Divide and check. Remember to estimate.

9. $6\overline{)43}$ 10. $5\overline{)83}$ 11. $9\overline{)89}$ 12. $4\overline{)66}$

13. $6\overline{)73}$ 14. $3\overline{)38}$ 15. $2\overline{)63}$ 16. $7\overline{)98}$

17. $4\overline{)59}$ 18. $7\overline{)90}$ 19. $4\overline{)85}$ 20. $9\overline{)179}$

21. $9\overline{)160}$ 22. $4\overline{)131}$ 23. $9\overline{)431}$ 24. $8\overline{)606}$

25. $6\overline{)366}$ 26. $7\overline{)511}$ 27. $6\overline{)407}$ 28. $9\overline{)852}$

29. $\frac{68}{9}$ ______ 30. $\frac{56}{3}$ ______ 31. $\frac{62}{2}$ ______

32. $\frac{85}{7}$ ______ 33. $\frac{73}{8}$ ______ 34. $\frac{91}{6}$ ______

35. $103 \div 9$ ______ 36. $471 \div 6$ ______ 37. $884 \div 7$ ______

38. $781 \div 7$ ______ 39. $537 \div 6$ ______ 40. $968 \div 6$ ______

Solve.

41. During a 6-hour radio show, the disc jockey wanted to play 71 songs. She played the same number of songs each hour. How many did she play during each hour? How many songs were left over for her next show?

______

42. The disc jockey played 78 songs during another 6-hour show. How many songs did she play each hour?

______

Name: ____________________

ZEROS IN THE QUOTIENT

Divide and check. Remember to estimate.

1. $6\overline{)64}$ **2.** $5\overline{)102}$ **3.** $9\overline{)367}$ **4.** $8\overline{)485}$

5. $4\overline{)123}$ **6.** $8\overline{)167}$ **7.** $5\overline{)254}$ **8.** $4\overline{)804}$

9. $3\overline{)921}$ **10.** $6\overline{)2,412}$ **11.** $7\overline{)769}$ **12.** $5\overline{)2,040}$

13. $7\overline{)2,128}$ **14.** $8\overline{)4,647}$ **15.** $7\overline{)2,242}$ **16.** $6\overline{)3,631}$

17. $3\overline{)1,680}$ **18.** $9\overline{)1,865}$ **19.** $8\overline{)2,807}$ **20.** $5\overline{)1,104}$

21. $\frac{2,418}{6} =$ ________ **22.** $\frac{686}{2}$ ________ **23.** $\frac{1,546}{7}$ ________

24. 1,525 ÷ 8 ________ **25.** 3,040 ÷ 5 ________ **26.** 727 ÷ 7 ________

27. 615 ÷ 2 ________ **28.** 1,982 ÷ 3 ________ **29.** 4,537 ÷ 9 ________

30. 286 ÷ 7 ________ **31.** 1,685 ÷ 6 ________ **32.** 974 ÷ 8 ________

33. 1,802 ÷ 3 ________ **34.** 3,544 ÷ 5 ________ **35.** 4,012 ÷ 4 ________

Solve.

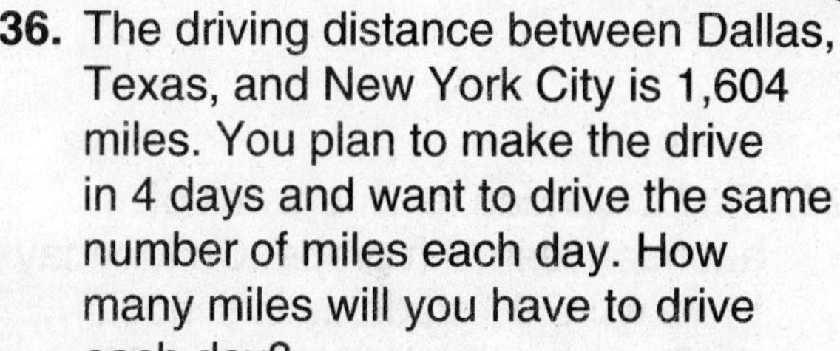

36. The driving distance between Dallas, Texas, and New York City is 1,604 miles. You plan to make the drive in 4 days and want to drive the same number of miles each day. How many miles will you have to drive each day?

____

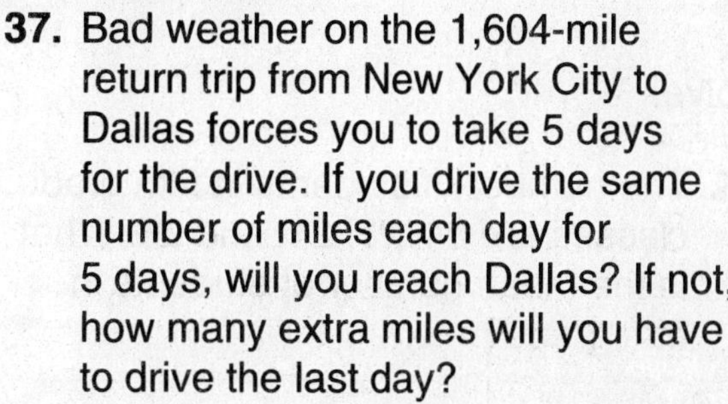

37. Bad weather on the 1,604-mile return trip from New York City to Dallas forces you to take 5 days for the drive. If you drive the same number of miles each day for 5 days, will you reach Dallas? If not, how many extra miles will you have to drive the last day?

____

Name: ______________________________

MEAN

Find the mean.

1. 2, 6, 5, 4, 3 ______

2. 6, 0, 8, 3, 3 ______

3. 8, 5, 7, 8, 2 ______

4. 9, 12, 12, 7 ______

5. 9, 13, 15, 11 ______

6. 20, 9, 10 ______

7. 20, 19, 27, 12, 27 ______

8. 16, 8, 12, 0 ______

9. \$2, \$5, \$3, \$6, \$9 ______

10. \$14, \$31, \$28, \$7 ______

11. 12, 0, 17, 31, 10 ______

12. 6, 7, 13, 0, 3, 13 ______

13. \$32, \$67, \$19, \$26 ______

14. 38, 45, 52, 29 ______

15. \$8, \$6, \$11, \$4, \$11 ______

16. 9, 12, 14, 23, 12 ______

17. 29, 37, 42, 51, 21 ______

18. 65, 57, 43, 72, 63 ______

19. 8, 7, 7, 8, 10 ______

20. 14, 17, 16, 15, 23 ______

21. 21, 33, 92, 46, 38 ______

22. 49, 63, 29, 43, 31 ______

23. 8, 6, 11, 10, 4, 7, 17 ______

24. 18, 12, 21, 31, 28, 17, 20 ______

Solve.

25. The number of students in fifth grade classes are 24, 25, 27, and 28. What is the mean number of students in fifth grade?

____

26. Find the mean for one week of attendance in fifth grade. On Monday there were 96 students in school. On Tuesday, 94; Wednesday, 88; Thursday, 90; and Friday, 92.

____

Name:

Problem-Solving Strategy: Use Alternate Solution Methods

✔ Read
✔ Plan
✔ Solve
✔ Look Back

Solve. Then identify an alternate solution method you could use to solve the problem.

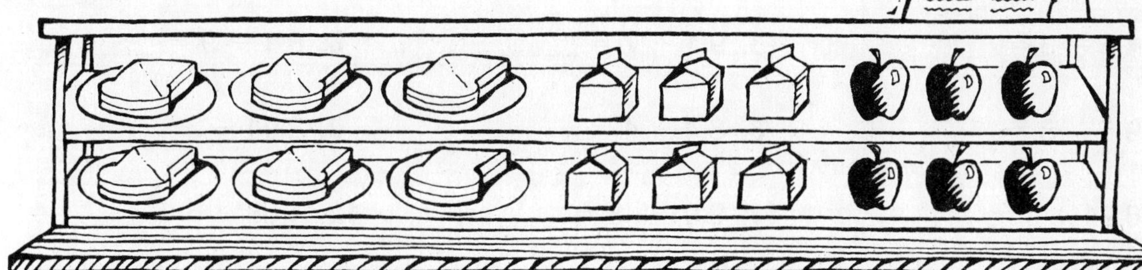

1. As part of a nutrition project, your class was asked to prepare the school lunches for the day. Your job was to make tuna and turkey sandwiches. You noticed that for every 4 tuna sandwiches you made, you made 7 turkey sandwiches. When you were done, you had made a total of 44 sandwiches. How many of each kind did you make?

2. On Monday, there is a choice of 3 sandwiches and 4 fruits. On Tuesday, students can choose from 2 sandwiches and 5 fruits. How many more choices do students have on Monday than on Tuesday if every student selects one sandwich and one fruit?

3. To make 120 tuna sandwiches, the school uses 12 pounds of canned tuna, 4 pounds of mayonnaise, and 8 loaves of bread. How much of each ingredient would be needed to make 30 tuna sandwiches?

4. The 3 lunch periods take a total of 2 hours and 20 minutes. If the first lunch period begins at 11:15 A.M., at what time does the third lunch period end?

Name: ______________________________

Use Models to Divide Decimals

Divide. You may use place-value models to help you.

1. 3.5 ÷ 5 = _____ **2.** 2.8 ÷ 7 = _____ **3.** 4.8 ÷ 6 = _____

4. 4.5 ÷ 3 = _____ **5.** 9.1 ÷ 7 = _____ **6.** 8.1 ÷ 9 = _____

7. 9.6 ÷ 8 = _____ **8.** 8.4 ÷ 4 = _____ **9.** 2.94 ÷ 3 = _____

10. 6.24 ÷ 4 = _____ **11.** 9.91 ÷ 3 = _____ **12.** 1.68 ÷ 6 = _____

13. 2)6.4 **14.** 5)8.5 **15.** 4)1.6 **16.** 2)3.8

17. 9)3.87 **18.** 7)9.17 **19.** 5)4.15 **20.** 5)6.75

21. 6)19.2 **22.** 3)4.71 **23.** 6)5.28 **24.** 4)10.56

Solve.

25. The quotient is 0.29. The divisor is 6.

What is the dividend? _______

26. The quotient is 1.16. The divisor is 4.

What is the dividend? _______

27. The divisor is 8. The quotient is 0.46.

What is the dividend? _______

28. The divisor is 7. The quotient is 0.66.

What is the dividend? _______

Is the quotient greater than or less than 1?

29. 1.6 ÷ 8 _______ **30.** 24 ÷ 8 _______ **31.** 0.49 ÷ 7 _______ **32.** 5.6 ÷ 8 _______

33. 42 ÷ 7 _______ **34.** 0.64 ÷ 8 _______ **35.** 3.26 ÷ 2 _______ **36.** 3.63 ÷ 3 _______

Name: ______________________________

Divide Decimals by Whole Numbers

Divide and check. Remember to estimate.

1. $5\overline{)5.1}$ **2.** $6\overline{)3.63}$ **3.** $8\overline{)5.64}$ **4.** $3\overline{)2.19}$

5. $5\overline{)5.63}$ **6.** $2\overline{)5.61}$ **7.** $4\overline{)3.22}$ **8.** $7\overline{)5.32}$

9. $6\overline{)9}$ **10.** $4\overline{)2.02}$ **11.** $9\overline{)\$8.01}$ **12.** $7\overline{)0.105}$

13. $12.6 \div 7$ **14.** $0.288 \div 6$ **15.** $6.72 \div 4$ **16.** $0.171 \div 3$

17. $\frac{29.56}{4}$ **18.** $\frac{7.506}{3}$ **19.** $\frac{3.368}{2}$ **20.** $\frac{\$43.74}{9}$

Find the mean.

21.

Hour	1:00	2:00	3:00	4:00
Customers	32	21	19	20

mean = ______________

22.

Customer	1	2	3	4	5
Amount Spent	$1.89	$2.49	$3.39	$2.09	$1.99

mean = ______________

Solve.

23. Mercy placed 5 identical cubes on a balance scale. A total of 36.25 grams of weight balanced with the cubes. How much did each cube weigh?

24. Three cubes of different weights balanced with a weight of 47.4 grams. What is the mean weight of the 3 cubes?

Name:

More Dividing Decimals

Divide and check.

1. $8\overline{)0.84}$
2. $7\overline{)9.1}$
3. $6\overline{)15}$
4. $7\overline{)21.14}$
5. $5\overline{)10.15}$
6. $9\overline{)27.36}$
7. $2\overline{)12.2}$
8. $4\overline{)12.2}$
9. $4\overline{)34.24}$
10. $5\overline{)3.9}$
11. $5\overline{)6.36}$
12. $5\overline{)45.25}$
13. $4\overline{)4.06}$
14. $5\overline{)5.3}$
15. $5\overline{)5.04}$
16. $7\overline{)\$13.58}$
17. 12 ÷ 5 ________
18. $5.34 ÷ 6 ________
19. 15.8 ÷ 4 ________
20. $30.30 ÷ 6 ________
21. 12.3 ÷ 5 ________
22. 64.28 ÷ 8 ________
23. 2.6 ÷ 4 ________
24. 70.93 ÷ 2 ________

Estimate and then divide. Round the quotient to the nearest hundredth.

25. $4\overline{)20.2}$
26. $8\overline{)16.2}$
27. $5\overline{)15.03}$
28. $6\overline{)4.23}$
29. $4\overline{)3.22}$
30. $6\overline{)48.15}$
31. $5\overline{)1.52}$
32. $6\overline{)18.81}$
33. $8\overline{)18.2}$
34. $4\overline{)12.86}$
35. $5\overline{)23.04}$
36. $5\overline{)35.02}$
37. $5\overline{)42.02}$
38. $4\overline{)12.08}$
39. $5\overline{)30.87}$
40. $5\overline{)4.56}$

Solve.

41. Students sold flowers to celebrate Earth Day. Annie sold 9 bunches of flowers and collected a total of $18.27. How much did she charge for each bunch of flowers? ________

42. Ken sold 4 bunches of flowers on each of the two days of the sale. He collected $12.24. How much did he charge for each bunch of flowers? ________

Name: ______________________________

Multiplication and Division Expressions

Evaluate the expression.

1. $3 \times a$ for $a = 7$ ________

2. $x \div 3$ for $x = 12$ ________

3. $m \div 5$ for $m = 75$ ________

4. $7 \times r$ for $r = 6$ ________

5. $36 \times h$ for $h = 3$ ________

6. $y \div 8$ for $y = 56$ ________

7. $c \div 3$ for $c = 39$ ________

8. $203 \times b$ for $b = 2$ ________

9. $z \div 8$ for $z = 448$ ________

10. $n \div 4$ for $n = 8.8$ ________

11. $27 \times m$ for $m = 3.2$ ________

12. $e \div 5$ for $e = 10.5$ ________

13. $d \div 6$ for $d = 45$ ________

14. $25 \times h$ for $h = 1.7$ ________

15. $r \div 2$ for $r = 3.5$ ________

16. $16.2 \div y$ for $y = 9$ ________

Algebra Complete the table.

17.

RULE: $m \div 4$	
Input	**Output**
24	
36	
26	
2	

18.

RULE: $n \times 6$	
Input	**Output**
8	
2.2	
5.8	
0.7	

Solve.

19. At Patty's Aquarium they put 8 tropical fish in each tank. Write an expression to show the number of tanks that can be filled with *x* goldfish. How many tanks can be filled with 96 tropical fish?

____

20. On Saturdays, an average of 27 customers come into the store each hour. Write an expression to show the number of customers that come into a store in *h* hours. How many customers would come into the store in 8 hours?

____

McGraw-Hill School Division

Name: ______________________

Problem Solving: Interpret the Quotient and Remainder

✔ Read
✔ Plan
✔ Solve
✔ Look Back

Solve.

1. All 195 fifth graders are going on a class field trip to Washington, D.C. They will be staying in a hotel near the White House. The rooms are set up for 6 students. How many rooms will be needed?

   ____

2. If each 6-person room is filled before another is opened, how many of the 195 students will be in the only room that is not full?

   ____

   ____

3. Five buses were rented for the trip. Each bus costs $300. If the school collected $10 from each of the 195 students going on the trip, would there be enough money for the buses? Explain how you decided.

   ____

   ____

   ____

4. At the Air and Space Museum, a space travel film that 40 students wanted to see was shown in a room that had seats for only 9 at a time. What is the least number of screenings that could include all of the students?

   ____

   ____

Solve using any method.

5. The bus trip back to school took 6 hours 30 minutes. If the students left at 7:45 A.M., how much before the 3:00 P.M. dismissal time did they arrive at school? __________

6. In the bookstore at the Air and Space Museum, the teachers wanted to buy 7 books for the school library. The prices were $14.95, $14.95, $19.95, $17.95, $13.95, $15.95, and $21.95. Was $150 enough to pay for the seven books? How did you decide?

   ____

   ____

   ____

7. The film took 10 minutes and there was a 10-minute period between showings. If the first of the 5 groups saw the 10:00 A.M. show, what time did the last group finish? __________

Name: ____________________

Mental Math: Use Division Patterns

Use mental math to complete the pattern.

1. 360 ÷ 60 = 6
   3,600 ÷ 60 = 60
   36,000 ÷ 60 = _____

2. 150 ÷ 50 = 3
   1,500 ÷ 50 = _____
   15,000 ÷ 50 = _____

3. 540 ÷ 90 = 6
   5,400 ÷ 90 = _____
   54,000 ÷ 90 = _____

4. 270 ÷ 90 = 3
   2,700 ÷ 90 = _____
   27,000 ÷ 90 = _____

5. 630 ÷ 70 = 9
   6,300 ÷ 70 = _____
   63,000 ÷ 70 = _____

6. 810 ÷ 90 = 9
   8,100 ÷ 90 = _____
   81,000 ÷ 90 = _____

7. 480 ÷ 80 = _____
   4,800 ÷ 80 = 60
   48,000 ÷ 80 = _____

8. 300 ÷ 60 = 5
   3,000 ÷ 60 = _____
   30,000 ÷ 60 = _____

9. 140 ÷ 20 = _____
   1,400 ÷ 20 = 70
   14,000 ÷ 20 = _____

10. 180 ÷ 60 = 3
    1,800 ÷ 60 = _____
    18,000 ÷ 60 = _____

11. 450 ÷ 90 = _____
    4,500 ÷ 90 = 50
    45,000 ÷ 90 = _____

12. 560 ÷ 70 = 8
    5,600 ÷ 70 = _____
    56,000 ÷ 70 = _____

Divide mentally.

13. 320 ÷ 80 = _____
14. 4,500 ÷ 50 = _____
15. 2,000 ÷ 50 = _____
16. 2,400 ÷ 60 = _____
17. 40,000 ÷ 50 = _____
18. 25,000 ÷ 50 = _____
19. $70\overline{)21{,}000}$
20. $80\overline{)16{,}000}$
21. $60\overline{)48{,}000}$
22. $90\overline{)63{,}000}$
23. $60\overline{)4{,}200}$
24. $70\overline{)28{,}000}$

Solve.

25. A stadium can hold 72,000 people in 80 sections of equal size. How many people can be seated in each section?

    ____

26. A baseball team plans to give away caps as gifts to people at the game. They ordered 18,000 caps. If 60 cartons are delivered, how many caps are in each carton?

    ____

Practice 50

Name:

MENTAL MATH: ESTIMATE QUOTIENTS

Estimate the quotient. Explain your method.

1. 295 ÷ 6 ________ 2. 647 ÷ 8 ________

3. 5,603 ÷ 89 ________ 4. 1,844 ÷ 27 ________

5. 3,886 ÷ 41 ________ 6. 4,852 ÷ 66 ________

7. 62,854 ÷ 92 ________ 8. 43,447 ÷ 56 ________

9. 73,901 ÷ 93 ________ 10. 24,106 ÷ 55 ________

11. 24,256 ÷ 22 ________ 12. 48,376 ÷ 74 ________

13. 39,111 ÷ 47 ________ 14. 11,886 ÷ 65 ________

15. 31,794 ÷ 45 ________ 16. 70,981 ÷ 83 ________

17. 67)20,098 ________ 18. 94)53,510 ________

19. 52)9,461 ________ 20. 68)2,490 ________

21. 19)4,098 ________ 22. 81)73,804 ________

23. 96)37,990 ________ 24. 66)19,583 ________

25. 62)35,003 ________ 26. 67)33,875 ________

27. 88)79,663 ________ 28. 56)46,008 ________

Solve.

29. A total of 1,652 valves were used for 73 cars as they were being assembled. About how many valves were used for each car?

____

30. Each of the 19 parking lots at an auto plant holds the same number of new cars. If there are 4,134 cars in the lots waiting to be shipped, about how many cars are in each lot?

____

Name:

USE MODELS TO DIVIDE

Divide. You may use place-value models.

1. 77 ÷ 12 = ______
2. 39 ÷ 14 = ______
3. 98 ÷ 21 = ______
4. 78 ÷ 26 = ______
5. 74 ÷ 22 = ______
6. 68 ÷ 19 = ______
7. 105 ÷ 17 = ______
8. 134 ÷ 22 = ______
9. 132 ÷ 33 = ______
10. 214 ÷ 43 = ______
11. 234 ÷ 55 = ______
12. 196 ÷ 56 = ______
13. 168 ÷ 31 = ______
14. 129 ÷ 18 = ______
15. 227 ÷ 39 = ______
16. 218 ÷ 67 = ______
17. 264 ÷ 44 = ______
18. 711 ÷ 41 = ______
19. 670 ÷ 25 = ______
20. 229 ÷ 15 = ______

21. 32)123
22. 40)204
23. 19)188
24. 20)176
25. 39)94
26. 23)142
27. 36)232
28. 18)111
29. 12)56
30. 13)155
31. 43)250
32. 22)228
33. 32)124
34. 29)243
35. 18)203
36. 40)210

Solve.

37. The dividend is 288 and the divisor is 44. What are the quotient and the remainder?

______

38. The dividend is 220 and the divisor is 28. What are the quotient and the remainder?

______

Name: ______

DIVIDE BY 2-DIGIT DIVISORS

Divide and check. Remember to estimate.

1. 44)145
2. 54)209
3. 33)120
4. 61)287
5. 49)186
6. 68)143
7. 71)228
8. 39)336
9. 72)654
10. 92)1,790
11. 58)4,880
12. 39)1,998
13. 88)2,755
14. 75)1,733
15. 49)3,975
16. 23)1,491
17. 44)3,510
18. 58)1,394
19. 82)2,298
20. 77)3,450
21. 1,700 ÷ 44 = ______
22. 2,008 ÷ 47 = ______
23. 3,651 ÷ 79 = ______
24. 1,352 ÷ 19 = ______
25. 1,656 ÷ 78 = ______
26. 2,390 ÷ 57 = ______
27. 1,776 ÷ 18 = ______
28. 2,110 ÷ 65 = ______
29. 3,900 ÷ 44 = ______
30. 2,764 ÷ 73 = ______
31. 1,487 ÷ 31 = ______
32. 1,720 ÷ 89 = ______

Solve.

33. Mike places an order at Jack's Hardware Store. He needs 1,890 nails. Jack knows there are 90 nails in a box. How many boxes of nails does Jack order for Mike?

______

34. Mike also needs 3,672 sheets of sandpaper. Sandpaper comes in packages of 68. How many packages will Mike need to order?

______

Name:

Problem-Solving Strategy: Guess, Test, and Revise

✔ Read
✔ Plan
✔ Solve
✔ Look Back

Solve using the guess, test, and revise strategy.

1. At the Sports Stop Catalog Company, an order comes in for 18 baseball hats. Some of the hats are $7 and some are $9. The order's total is $142. How many hats are $9 hats?

2. Justin, a telephone operator, worked 5 hours longer than Rosie, another telephone operator. The product of the number of hours they worked is 66. How many hours did Rosie work?

3. There are 141 items to choose from in the catalog. There are twice as many pieces of equipment as there are clothing items. How many pieces of equipment are in the catalog?

4. While placing an order, Kate notices that the product of the page numbers on the two facing pages is 420. What are the page numbers?

Solve using any method. Use the price list for problems 7–8.

5. At the factory, tennis balls are packed 3 to a can. In one hour, 1,315 balls are produced. How many cans were filled? How many tennis balls were left?

6. A nearby golf academy calls and orders 500 boxes of golf balls. Each box contains 18 golf balls. How many golf balls did the academy order?

7. The price list shows the cost of several items at the Sports Stop. Alfredo bought 5 items and spent $79.87. What did Alfredo buy?

8. Rolanda has $100 to replace school gym equipment. She calls the Sports Stop to buy a basketball and as many baseball bats as possible. What is the greatest number of baseball bats that she can buy if she also buys a basketball?

Price List

Can of tennis balls	$ 2.89
Basketball	$42.49
Baseball bat	$15.80

Name:

Practice 54

DIVIDE GREATER NUMBERS

Divide and check. Remember to estimate.

1. 91)5,412
2. 78)3,488
3. 42)3,450
4. 56)5,966
5. 29)26,204
6. 54)16,453
7. 42)12,819
8. 70)49,201
9. 39)15,843
10. 62)19,030
11. 33)10,198
12. 42)96,878
13. 37)189,008
14. 54)362,289
15. 75)97,665

16. 5,810 ÷ 87 = ________
17. 4,807 ÷ 68 = ________
18. 2,990 ÷ 71 = ________
19. 5,215 ÷ 53 = ________
20. $9,752 ÷ 46 = ________
21. 6,720 ÷ 45 = ________
22. 7,921 ÷ 49 = ________
23. 9,218 ÷ 81 = ________
24. $15,443 ÷ 29 = ________
25. 75,006 ÷ 83 = ________
26. $13,690 ÷ 54 = ________
27. 60,801 ÷ 92 = ________

Solve.

28. Members of the Bladerunners skating club collected $4,320 from car washes, raffles, and donations. They want to buy Ultrablade skates which are $89 a pair. How many pairs of skates will they be able to buy?

____

29. During their first month of skating, 29 members of the Bladerunners covered a total of 1,624 miles. What was the average number of miles skated by each member?

____

Name: ______

Divide by Powers of 10

Complete the pattern mentally.

1. 3,276 ÷ 10 = 327.6
3,276 ÷ 100 = ______
3,276 ÷ 1,000 = ______

2. 629 ÷ 10 = ______
629 ÷ 100 = ______
629 ÷ 1,000 = ______

3. 2,065 ÷ 10 = ______
2,065 ÷ 100 = ______
2,065 ÷ 1,000 = ______

4. 138 ÷ 10 = ______
138 ÷ 100 = ______
138 ÷ 1,000 = ______

5. 50 ÷ 10 = ______
50 ÷ 100 = ______
50 ÷ 1,000 = ______

6. 147.2 ÷ 10 = ______
147.2 ÷ 100 = ______
147.2 ÷ 1,000 = ______

7. 23.8 ÷ 10 = ______
23.8 ÷ 100 = ______
23.8 ÷ 1,000 = ______

8. 9.2 ÷ 10 = ______
9.2 ÷ 100 = ______
9.2 ÷ 1,000 = ______

9. 7.6 ÷ 10 = ______
7.6 ÷ 100 = ______
7.6 ÷ 1,000 = ______

Divide mentally.

10. 267 ÷ 10 = ______

11. 58 ÷ 100 = ______

12. 4.5 ÷ 10 = ______

13. $15 ÷ 100 = ______

14. 32.98 ÷ 10 = ______

15. 8 ÷ 10 = ______

16. 9.02 ÷ 10 = ______

17. 300 ÷ 1,000 = ______

18. 68 ÷ 1,000 = ______

19. 8.4 ÷ 1,000 = ______

20. 32 ÷ 1,000 = ______

21. 40.3 ÷ 100 = ______

22. 1.2 ÷ 100 = ______

23. 6 ÷ 1,000 = ______

24. 5.6 ÷ 100 = ______

25. 54.2 ÷ 1,000 = ______

26. 1.9 ÷ 100 = ______

27. 2 ÷ 1,000 = ______

28. 7.7 ÷ 10 = ______

29. 2.3 ÷ 1,000 = ______

Name: ______________________ Practice 56

DIVIDE BY 2-DIGIT NUMBERS

Divide.

1. $27\overline{)13.77}$ 2. $23\overline{)32.2}$ 3. $28\overline{)47.6}$ 4. $23\overline{)15.64}$

5. $66\overline{)27.72}$ 6. $45\overline{)8.55}$ 7. $12\overline{)28.32}$ 8. $14\overline{)27.02}$

9. $25\overline{)0.4}$ 10. $36\overline{)1.8}$ 11. $14\overline{)3.5}$ 12. $62\overline{)31.0}$

13. $70\overline{)1.05}$ 14. $40\overline{)6.48}$ 15. $95\overline{)4.56}$ 16. $50\overline{)9.4}$

17. $26.68 \div 23 =$ ________ 18. $76.32 \div 18 =$ ________

19. $91.7 \div 35 =$ ________ 20. $67.32 \div 22 =$ ________

21. $60.35 \div 17 =$ ________ 22. $66.56 \div 32 =$ ________

Divide. Round the quotient to the nearest hundredth or cent.

23. $20\overline{)51.24}$ 24. $25\overline{)76.6}$ 25. $40\overline{)\$51.4}$ 26. $53\overline{)44.4}$

Solve.

27. Twelve students each ordered a different meal from a fast-food restaurant as part of a science project. When they finished eating, they weighed all the packaging. They found that the packaging weighed a total of 2.88 pounds. What was the average weight of the packaging from each meal?

____

28. Later in the year the same 12 students repeated the experiment. The total weight of the same order this time was 2.16 pounds. What was the new average weight of the packaging?

____

Practice 57

Name:

Problem Solving: Use Alternate Solution Methods

✔ Read
✔ Plan
✔ Solve
✔ Look Back

Solve. Then identify an alternate solution you could use to solve the problem.

1. Your job as a volunteer at the public library is to shelve books that have been returned. You notice that for every 3 children's books, there are 8 adult books. When you finish, you put away a total of 66 books. How many of each type of book did you put away?

2. On Tuesdays, children can choose one of 4 videos and one of 2 story times. On Thursdays, children can choose one of 5 videos and one of 3 story times. How many more combinations are possible on Thursday than on Tuesday?

3. On a busy day the library collected $23.40. Eleven dollars was for the price of a lost book. The rest was in collected late fees. One late fee was $3. The person's book was a month overdue. The remaining money was from 47 people whose books were all two days late. How much is the overdue charge per day?

4. You are asked to unpack and place books in order on a special shelf. As you do this you notice a pattern: number 1 best seller, 15 copies; number 4 best seller, 13 copies; number 7 best seller, 11 copies. If the pattern continues how many copies were ordered for the number 22 best seller?

Solve using any method.

5. Iris has a 135-page book to read. She has 7 days to read the entire book. She has decided to read 20 pages each night for the first 6 nights. How many pages will she have to read on the seventh night to finish the book on time?

6. The school library received a carton of 22 new books. There were 18 history books and 7 music books. How many of the books were about the history of music?

Name: ______________________

Practice 58

Customary Length

Measure the line segment to the nearest $\frac{1}{2}$ inch, $\frac{1}{4}$ inch, $\frac{1}{8}$ inch, and $\frac{1}{16}$ inch.

1. ______________________

2. ______________________

3. ______________________

4. ______________________

5. ______________________

Which unit would you use to measure? Write *in., ft, yd,* or *mi.*

6. width of a sheet of paper ________

7. height of a giraffe

8. length of an aircraft carrier ________

9. distance from your home to France ________

10. length of a worm ________

11. height of a redwood tree ________

12. height of a basketball player ________

13. width of a computer disk ________

14. deepest part of an ocean ________

15. distance you can throw a ball

16. height of Mt. Denali ________

17. length of your arm ________

18. Draw a picture using line segments that are $2\frac{1}{2}$ in., $1\frac{3}{4}$ in., $\frac{5}{8}$ in., and $2\frac{5}{16}$ in. long.

Name: ______________________________

Customary Capacity and Weight

Which unit of capacity would you use to measure?
Write *c, pt, qt,* or *gal.*

1. drinking glass ______________

2. child's play pool ______________

3. large spaghetti pot ______________

4. kitchen sink ______________

5. can of paint ______________

6. bowl of soup ______________

7. plastic garbage bag ______________

8. bottle of soda ______________

9. small carton of milk ______________

10. coffee mug ______________

11. kitchen trash bin ______________

12. bottle of shampoo ______________

Which unit of weight would you use to measure? Write *oz, lb,* or *T.*

13. bicycle ________

14. minivan ________

15. box of staples ________

16. cruise ship ________

17. double CD ________

18. 5,000 pennies ________

19. backpack full of books ________

20. gorilla ________

21. carrot sticks ________

22. bowling ball ________

23. portable computer ________

24. pair of socks ________

Solve.

25. Kate brought 1,000 pennies in 20 rolls to the bank. Did they weigh closer to 6 ounces or 6 pounds?

____

26. Daniel was making a cake from a recipe he saw on television. He could not remember how much flour he needed. Did he most likely need 2 cups or 2 quarts of flour?

____

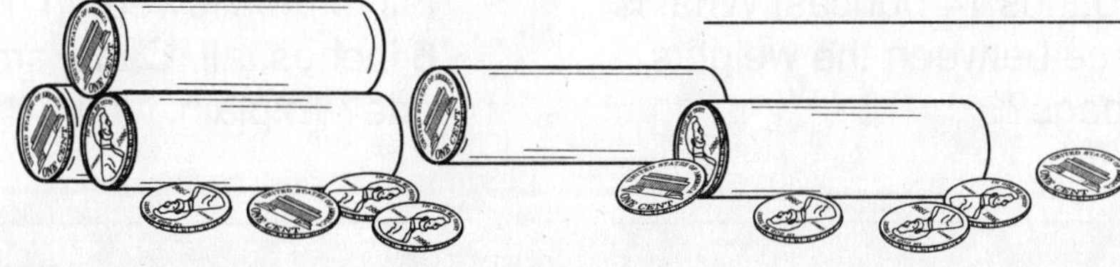

Name: ______________________________

UNDERSTANDING THE CUSTOMARY SYSTEM

Complete.

1. 36 in. = ________ ft
2. 18 yd = ________ ft
3. 3 gal = ________ qt
4. 14 pt = ________ qt
5. 16 qt = ________ gal
6. 48 in. = ________ ft
7. 2 mi = ________ ft
8. 6 gal = ________ pt
9. 8 lb = ________ oz
10. 6 ft = ________ in.
11. 48 in. = ________ ft
12. 36 qt = 9 ________
13. 1,000 ________ = $\frac{1}{2}$ T
14. 21 qt = ________ pt
15. 3 lb = 48 ________
16. 2 T = 4,000 ________
17. 216 ft = 72 ________
18. 96 oz = 6 ________
19. 55 in. = ________ ft ________ in.
20. 6 c = ________ qt ________ pt
21. 11 pt = ________ qt ________ pt
22. 27 oz = ________ lb ________ oz
23. 8 ft = ________ yd ________ ft
24. 3,000 lb = ________ T ________ lb

Add or subtract.

25. 3 gal 1 qt
+ 5 gal 2 qt
26. 9 yd 1 ft
+ 2 yd 6 ft
27. 12 yd 2 ft
− 8 yd 1 ft
28. 6 ft 4 in.
− 4 ft 8 in.
29. 1 qt 3 c
+ 5 qt 2 c
30. 12 lb 4 oz
− 10 lb 8 oz
31. 3 T
− 2 T 700 lb
32. 1 mi 2,500 ft
+ 7 mi 3,500 ft
33. 4 yd 1 ft
− 2 ft

Solve.

34. One bag of apples weighs 3 pounds 1 ounce. Another bag of apples weighs 2 pounds 14 ounces. What is the difference between the weights of the two bags?

____

35. An amusement park ride has a sign saying that you must be 53 inches tall to be allowed on. Ramon is 4 feet 8 inches tall. Can Ramon go on the ride? Explain.

____

Name: _______________ **Practice 61**

Problem-Solving Strategy: Find a Pattern

✔ Read
✔ Plan
✔ Solve
✔ Look Back

Solve using the find-a-pattern strategy.

1. The most popular exhibit at the Science Museum is the dinosaurs. For every 2 people who visit the Electricity Center, 7 visit the dinosaurs. How many people visit the dinosaurs if 20 people visit the Electricity Center?

   ____

2. Bill is designing a rock display for the museum. He put 63 rocks in the first row, 54 rocks in the second row, and 45 rocks in the third row. If the pattern continues, how many rocks does he use in the sixth row?

   ____

3. Wendy makes gift cards to sell in the museum store. She charges $5.50 for a box of 12 cards, $6.25 for a box of 24 cards, and $7 for a box of 36 cards. If this pattern continues, how much does she charge for a box of 72 cards?

   ____

4. When you get to the museum you realize there are 9 exhibits you want to see. You spend 15 minutes at the first exhibit. At every other exhibit, you spend 10 minutes more than you did at the one before it. How much time will you spend at the last exhibit?

   ____

Solve using any method.

5. Charlotte wants a bicycle that costs $199.00. She can make a down payment of $50.00 and pay $15 per month after that. Can she pay for the bicycle in one year? Explain how you decided.

   ____

6. Today is Saturday. What day of the week will it be
   a. 7 days from now? _______
   b. 21 days from now? _______
   c. 27 days from now? _______
   d. 80 days from now? _______

7. Allen's team scored 18 points in the first quarter of a basketball game, 15 points in the second, and 21 points in the third. The team's total score for the game was 71. How many points did they score in the fourth quarter?

   ____

8. Mrs. Gould sees a board game for $21.50, a word game for $14, a crafts kit for $29.95, and a video game for $42. Her budget is $120. Can she buy one of each? How did you decide?

   ____

Name: ____________________

METRIC LENGTH

Measure to the nearest *cm* and to the nearest *mm*.

1.

____

2.

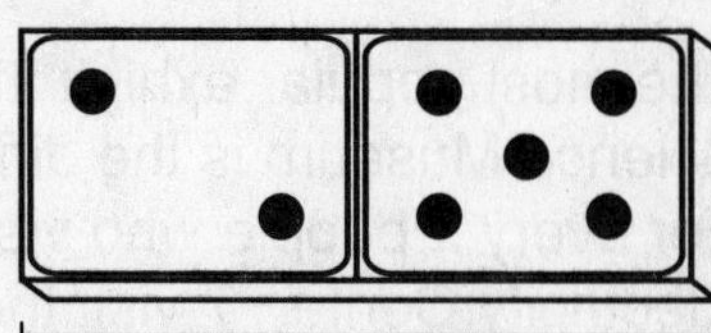

____

3.

____

4.

____

Draw a line segment with the given length.

5. 35 mm

6. 9 cm

7. 1 dm

8. 6 cm

Which unit would you use to measure? Write *mm, cm, dm, m,* or *km.*

9. length of your arm ________

10. length of a canoe ________

11. thickness of a penny ________

12. height of a diving board ________

13. length of a shoebox ________

14. altitude of a plane ________

15. thickness of an encyclopedia ________

16. height of your school ________

17. thickness of a rubber band ________

18. length of a bath towel ________

19. distance of a running race ________

20. height of a mountain ________

Name: ______________________________

Metric Capacity and Mass

Which unit of capacity would you use to measure? Write *mL* or *L.*

1. soup ladle ________
2. garden watering can ________
3. water glass ________
4. soup bowl ________
5. bathtub ________
6. ice cream cone ________
7. coffee cup ________
8. bucket ________
9. jam jar ________
10. baby bottle ________

Which unit of mass would you use to measure? Write *mg, g,* or *kg.*

11. calculator ________
12. brick ________
13. refrigerator ________
14. sheet of notepaper ________
15. sandwich ________
16. feather ________
17. puppy ________
18. dime ________
19. magazine ________
20. microwave ________

Solve.

21. A bag of rice contains 1,265 grams. About how many kilograms is that?

    ____

22. Barney made 1,800 mL of lemonade. About how many liters is that?

    ____

Practice 64

Name: ______________________________

UNDERSTANDING THE METRIC SYSTEM

Complete.

1. 70 mm = ________ cm
2. 19 m = ________ cm
3. 1.2 L = ________ mL
4. 670 m = ________ km
5. 120 mL = ________ L
6. 7 g = ________ mg
7. 2.7 kg = ________ g
8. 1.3 km = ________ m
9. 0.5 g = ________ mg
10. 2.8 cm = ________ mm
11. 390 mg = ________ g
12. 1,560 g = ________ kg
13. 2,800 mL = ________ L
14. 24 m = ________ cm
15. 320 cm = ________ m
16. 25 L = ________ mL
17. 1,200 mm = ________ cm
18. 34 cm = ________ mm

Add or subtract.

19. 650 g + 2 kg + 195 g

____

20. 8 L − 2,800 mL

____

21. 580 m + 1.2 km + 7 km

____

22. 68 cm − 320 mm

____

Solve.

23. Jodie has 0.5 liter of milk to use in two recipes. Each recipe uses 300 mL. Does she have enough? Explain.

____

____

24. A tunnel will be 1.3 kilometers long when completed. The workers have already completed 825 meters. How much remains to be built?

____

____

Name: ______________________________

TIME

Complete.

1. 48 mo = ________ y

2. 12 wk = ________ d

3. 360 s = ________ min

4. 245 d = ________ wk

5. 17 h = ________ min

6. 576 h = ________ d

7. 312 wk = ________ y

8. 96 mo = ________ y

9. 540 min = ________ h

10. 71 mo = ________ y ________ mo

11. 83 min = ________ h ________ min

12. 23 d = ________ wk ________ d

13. 7 yr 3 mo = ________ mo

14. 5 h 25 min = ________ min

15. 15.5 h = ________ min

16. 14 y 8 mo = ________ mo

Find the elapsed time.

17. from 2:20 A.M. to 9:55 A.M.

____

18. from 8:45 P.M. to 11:06 P.M.

____

19. from 10:50 A.M. to 1:45 P.M.

____

20. from 7:32 P.M. to 2:22 A.M.

____

21. from 3:15 P.M. to 9:03 P.M.

____

22. from 11:09 P.M. to 4:27 A.M.

____

Solve.

23. The bus trip from New York City to Boston takes 4 hours, 15 minutes. If you must be in Boston by 1:00 P.M., can you take a bus that leaves at 8:30 A.M.? What time will the bus arrive?

____

24. The ride from the bus station to downtown takes 35 minutes by taxicab. If you are meeting a friend at 2:30 P.M. and want to arrive by 2:20 P.M., what is the latest you should be in the taxi?

____

Practice 66

Name: ____________________

Problem Solving: Find Extra or Needed Information

✔ Read
✔ Plan
✔ Solve
✔ Look Back

Solve. Identify any extra information.

1. OmegaMan II was brought out soon after OmegaMan. Three dozen were shipped to your video store. The price of OmegaMan II was $9.25 more than OmegaMan. Together the two games cost $88.25. How much did each game cost?

____

____

2. Members of the video game club were asked to rate OmegaMan II. The results are shown below. The highest score they could give was 100. What was the median score given to OmegaMan II?

Stem	Leaf
6	89
7	035
8	15588
9	00022

____

3. In a video game tournament, Jeffrey defeated Carla by a total of 62,500 points. If they each played 10 games, about how many points did Jeffrey average per game? What information do you need to solve this problem? What information is extra?

____

____

____

4. Dana has twice as many video games as her brother. She needs $189 to buy a game system. She can waitress 8 hours per week and earn $5.50 per hour. Or she can baby-sit 10 hours per week and earn $4.00 per hour. Which job should she choose to reach $189 as quickly as possible?

____

____

____

Solve using any method.
Use the chart to solve problems 5–6.

Popcorn	
5 lb	$2.19
10 lb	$3.89
25 lb	$7.99

5. You have $20 to spend on popcorn. What is the greatest number of pounds you can buy? How much money will you have left after buying that amount?

____

6. Your job is to buy refreshments for the tournament. How much will you save if you buy a 25-lb bag of popcorn rather than two 10-lb bags and one 5-lb bag?

____

Name: ______________________________

POLYGONS

Identify the figure as *open* or *closed*.

1. 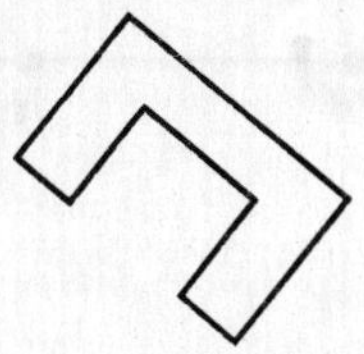
______

2. 
______

3. 
______

4. 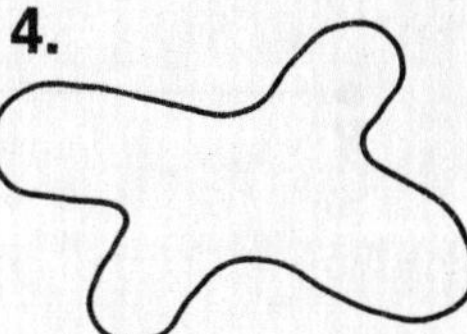
______

Match the figure with its name.

open figure	triangle	quadrilateral
pentagon	hexagon	octagon

5. 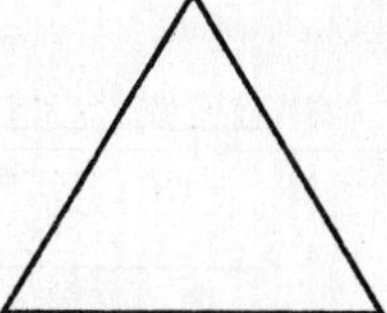
______

6. 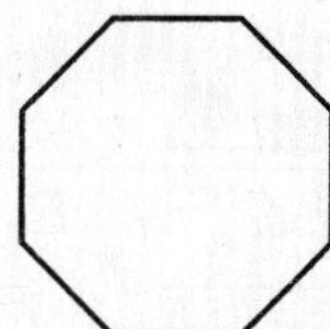
______

7. 
______

8. 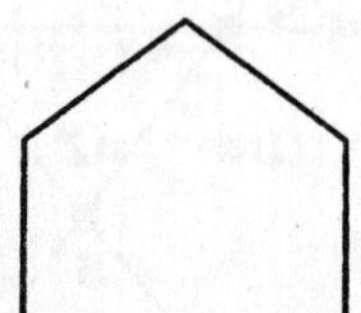
______

9. 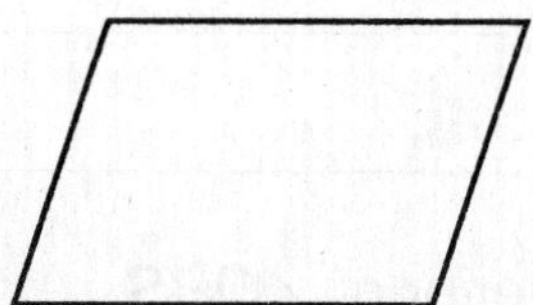
______

10. 
______

Use the box at the right for exercises 11–13.

Which figures are:

11. hexagons? ______

12. quadrilaterals? ______

13. regular triangles? ______

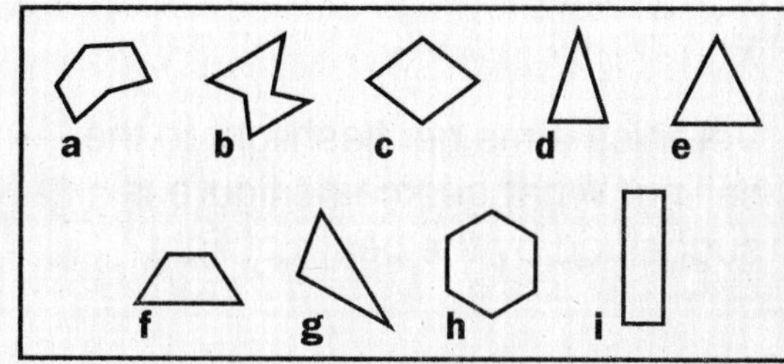

Name: ______________________ **Practice 68**

LANGUAGE OF GEOMETRY

Identify the figure. Then name it using symbols.

1. **2.**

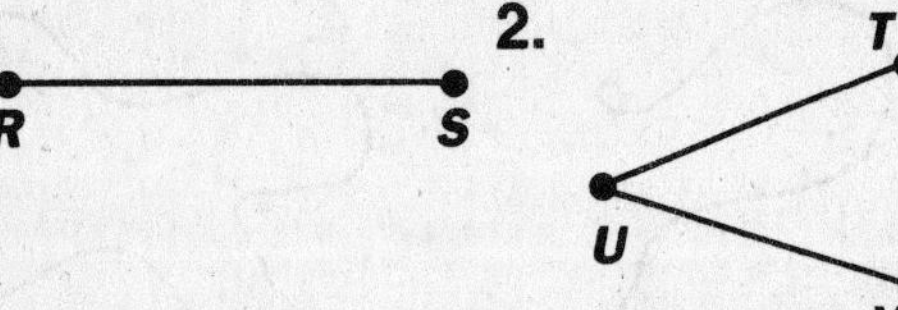

3.

Q

4.

5.

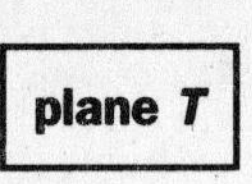

6.

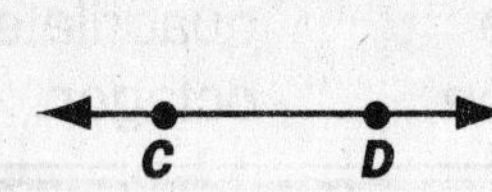

7.

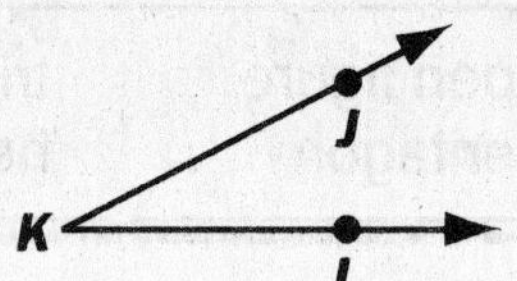

8.

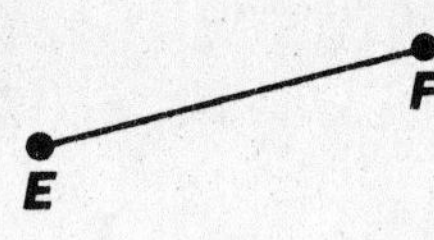

Use the diagram for exercises 9–12.

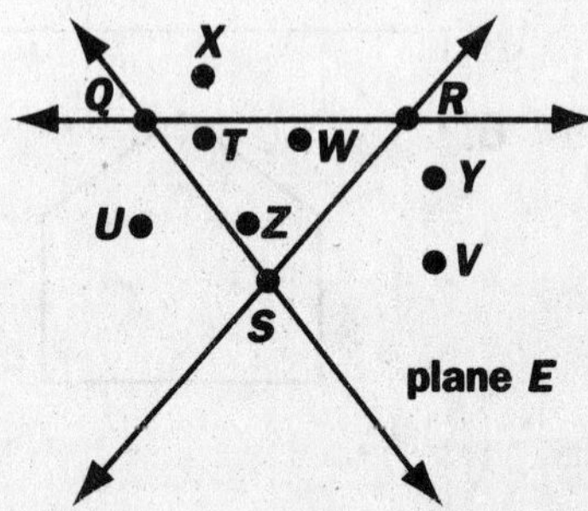

9. Name all the line segments. ______________

10. Name all the points. ______________

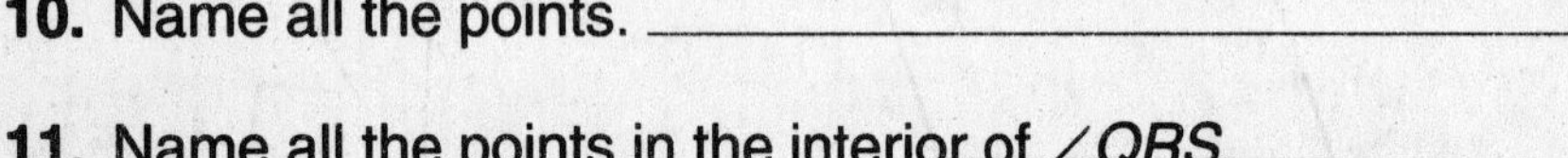

11. Name all the points in the interior of $\angle QRS$. ______________

12. Name all the points in the exterior of $\angle QRS$. ______________

13. Name the sides of $\angle QRS$. ______________

14. What plane do the lines lie in? ______________

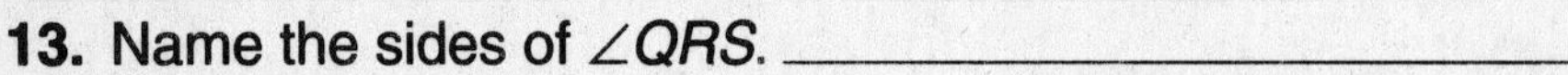

Solve.

15. Veronica aims her flashlight to the ceiling. What geometric figure is suggested by the beam of light?

____

16. What geometric figure is suggested by the hands of Veronica's clock at 3:00 P.M.?

____

Name: ____________________

Angles and Lines

Identify the angle as *acute, right, obtuse,* or *straight.* Then estimate the measure of the angles. Use a protractor to check your estimate.

1. 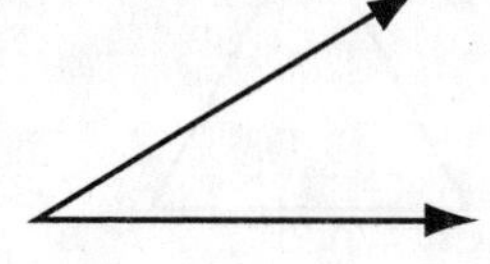

2. 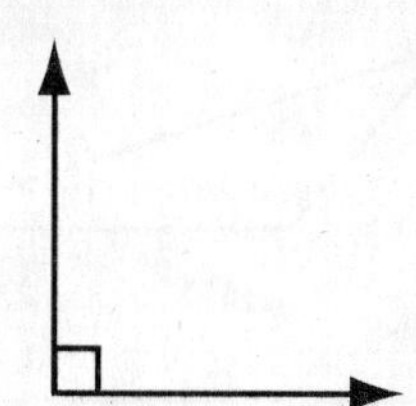

3. 

4. 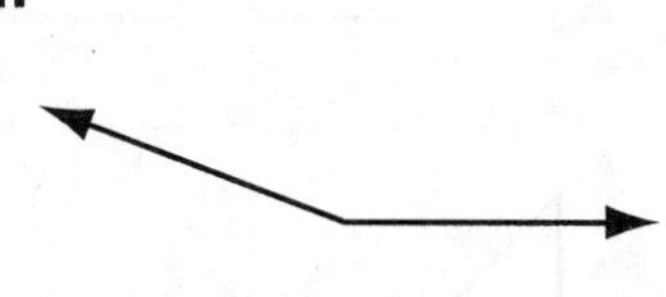

5. 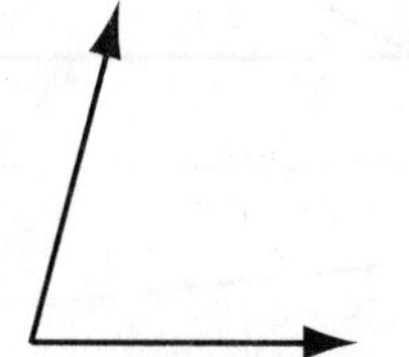

6. 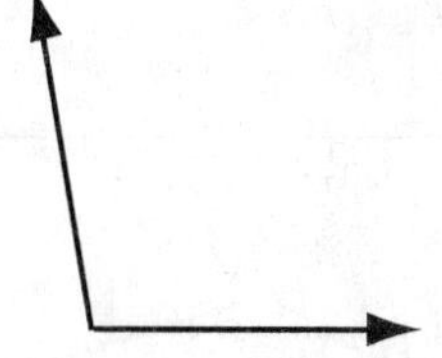

Name the pair of lines as *intersecting, parallel,* or *perpendicular.*

7. 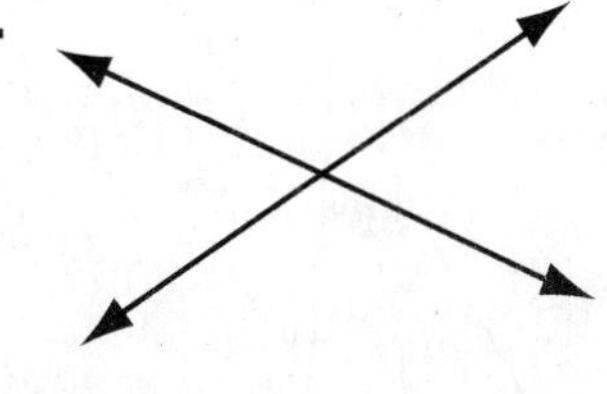

8. 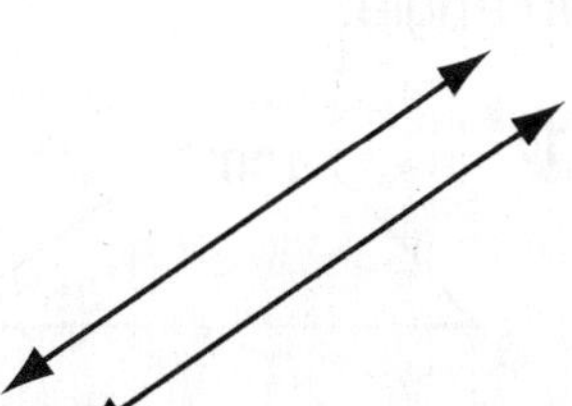

9. 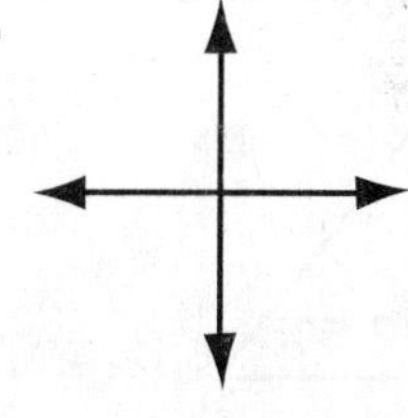

Solve.

10. Third Avenue and Ninth Street cross each other, making angles of 75° and 105°. What type of lines are suggested by these streets?

11. Third Avenue and Fifteenth Street are perpendicular to each other. What type of angle is formed where these streets meet?

Name: ______________________

TRIANGLES

Identify the triangle as *equilateral, isosceles,* or *scalene* and *right, acute,* or *obtuse.*

1. 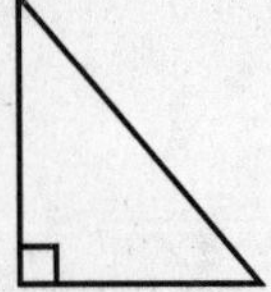

____

2. 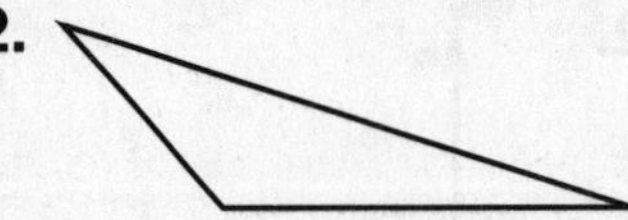

____

3. 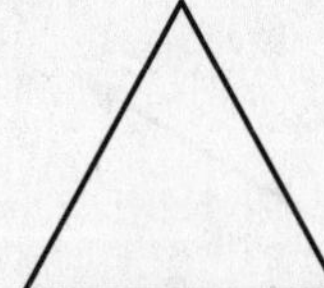

____

4. 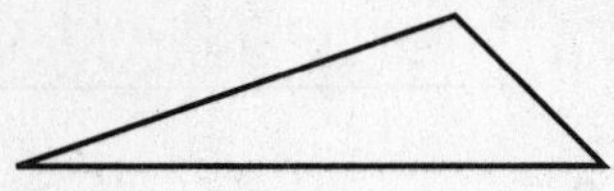

____

5. 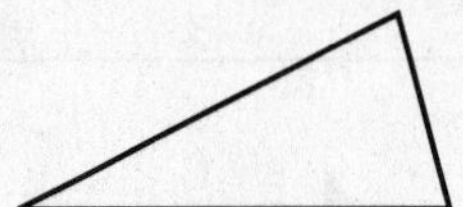

____

6. 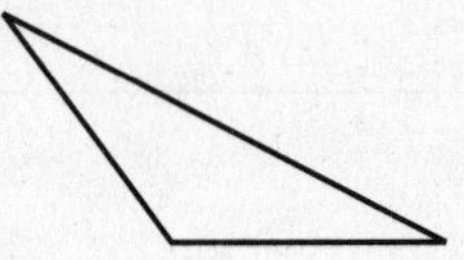

____

7. 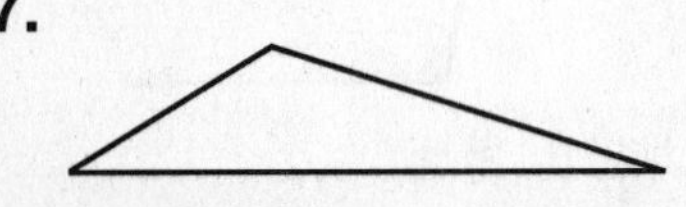

____

8. 

____

9. 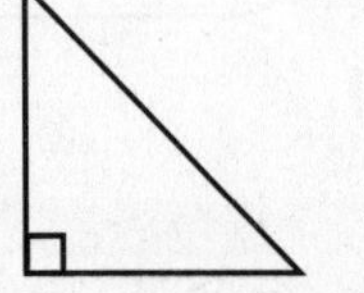

____

Find the measure of the unknown angle.

10. 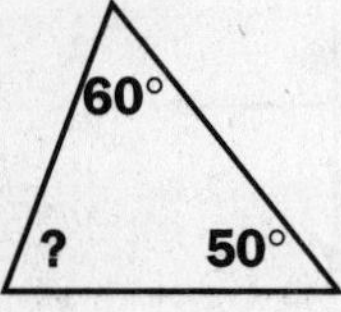

____

11. 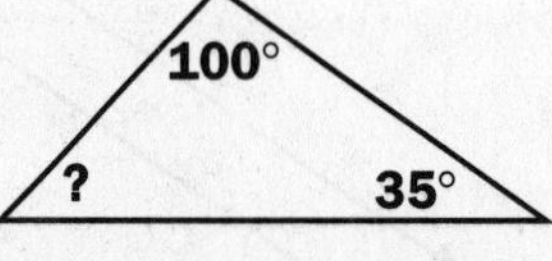

____

12. 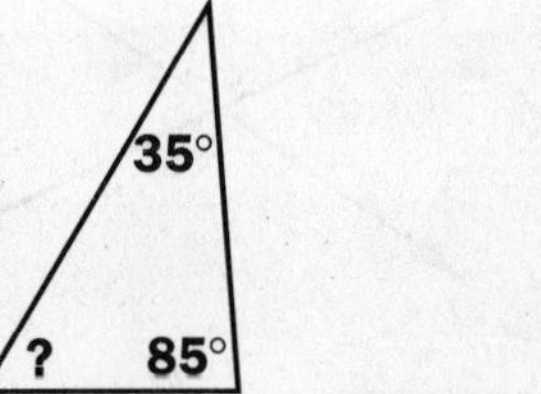

____

13. 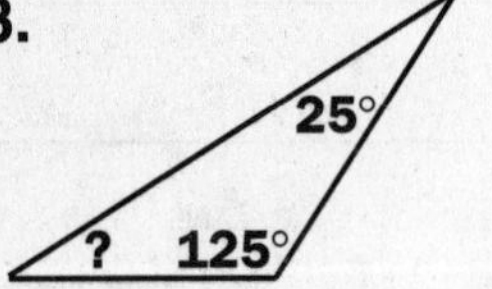

____

14. 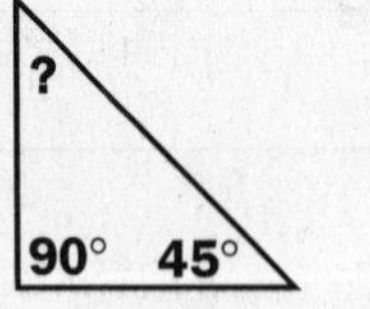

____

15. 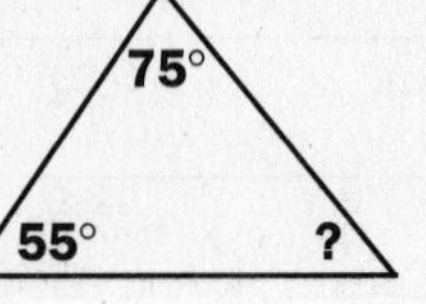

____

16. 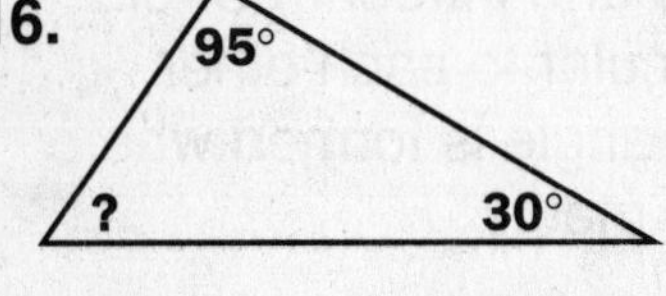

____

17. 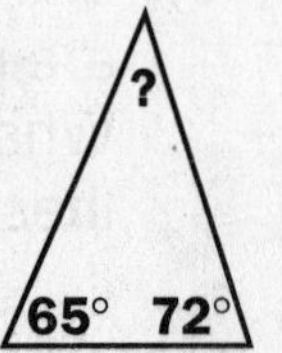

____

18. 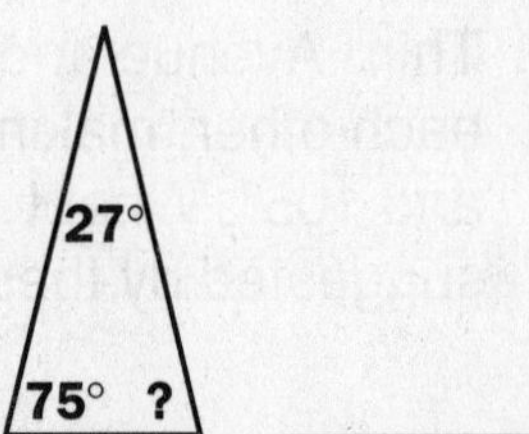

____

Name: ______________________________

QUADRILATERALS

Write the name that best fits the quadrilateral.

1. 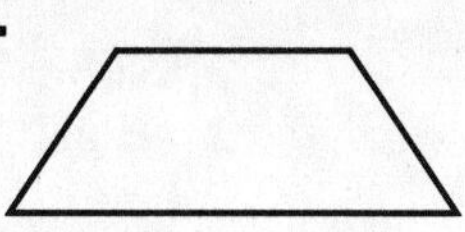

____

2. 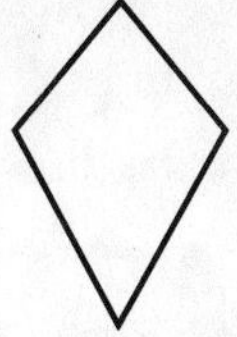

____

3. 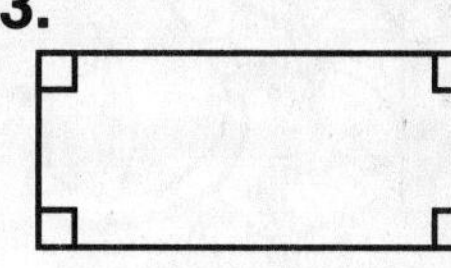

____

4. 

____

5. 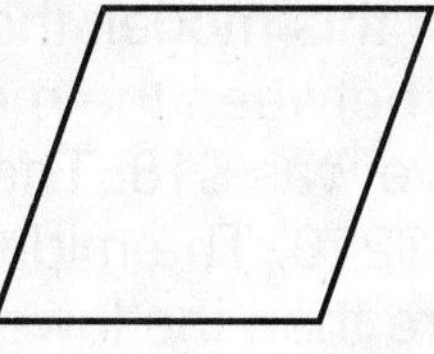

____

6. 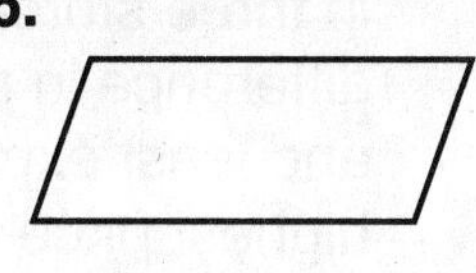

____

7. 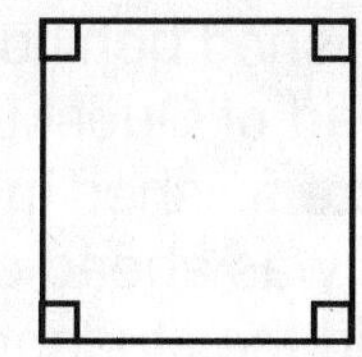

____

8. 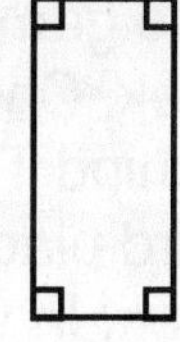

____

Find the measure of the unknown angle.

9. 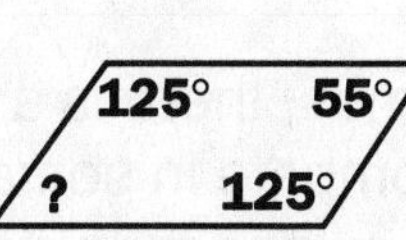

____

10. 100° 90° ? 90°

____

11. 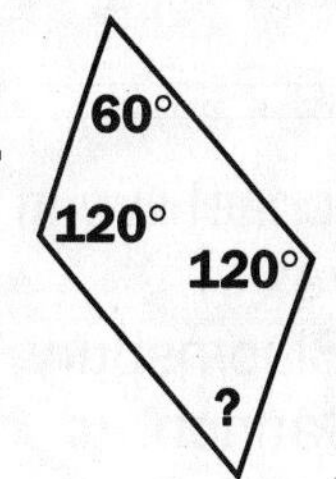

____

12. 110° 90° ? 80°

____

13. 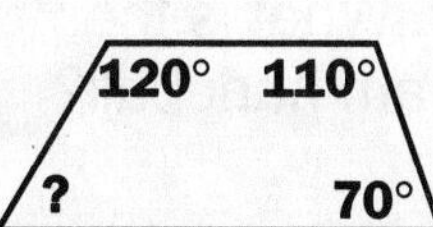

____

14. 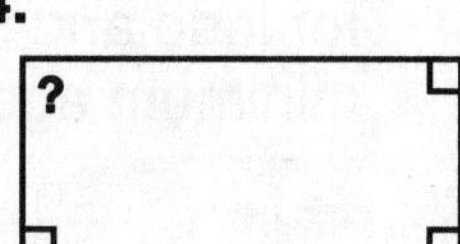

____

15. 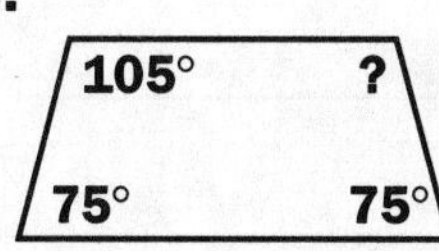

____

16. ? 120° 105° 60°

____

Write *true* or *false*. Explain your reasoning.

17. All rectangles are squares. ______________________________

____

18. Every trapezoid is a rhombus. ______________________________

____

Practice 72

Name: ______________________

Problem-Solving Strategy: Use Logical Reasoning

✔ Read
✔ Plan
✔ Solve
✔ Look Back

Solve using logical reasoning.

1. Students participated in a survey to rate games. Quest finished behind Trek. Chess was ahead of Quest but behind Trek. Star Gaze finished in third place. Checkers was ahead of Trek. In what order did the students rate the games?

____

____

2. Angel compared the price of a stereo in three stores. For this model, the difference in price between the most and least expensive was $18. The highest price was $220. The middle price was $10 more than the lowest price. What were the prices of the stereo at the three stores?

____

3. Charles, Omar, and Michael live in different towns. One lives in Appleton, one lives in Bloomsbury, and the other lives in Cannon. Michael does not live in Bloomsbury. Charles travels to Cannon to visit Omar. Where does each live?

____

____

4. In the Olympic Games, there is a minimum age to compete in some sports. The minimum age for judo is 15. For soccer you must be 23 or older. The minimum age for team handball is one year younger than the average of the age requirements for judo and soccer. What is the minimum age for team handball?

____

Solve using any method.

5. Marjorie Gestring was the youngest Olympics competitor to ever win a gold medal. She was 13 when she won for diving in 1936. How many years before the 2000 Olympics was she born?

____

6. Alex saw the FX87 CD player advertised for $179.95. This was $30.55 less than the highest price he had seen for the same model. How much was the highest price?

____

Name: ______________________________

CIRCLES

Identify the parts of Circle *O*.

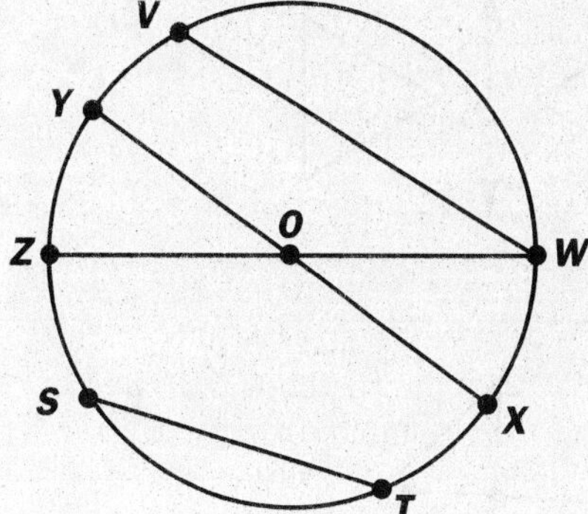

1. center ____________________
2. radii ____________________
3. chords ____________________
4. diameters ____________________
5. central angles ____________________

____

Solve. Use Circle *O*.

6. If $\overline{OX}$ = 6 in., how long is $\overline{YX}$? ____________
7. What is the measure of ∠*YOX*? ____________
8. If $\overline{XY}$ = 24 ft, how long is $\overline{OZ}$? ____________
9. If the measure of ∠*YOZ* is 50°, what is the measure of ∠*WOX*? ____________
10. If the measure of $\overline{OW}$ is 9 in., what is the measure of $\overline{YX}$? ____________
11. If the measure of ∠*YOW* is 140°, what is the measure of ∠*ZOX*? ____________

Write *true* or *false*. Explain your reasoning.

12. All chords are diameters. ____________________

____

____

13. All diameters are chords. ____________________

____

____

Name: ______

Practice 74

CONGRUENCE AND MOTION

Write whether a *slide, flip,* or *turn* was made.

1. 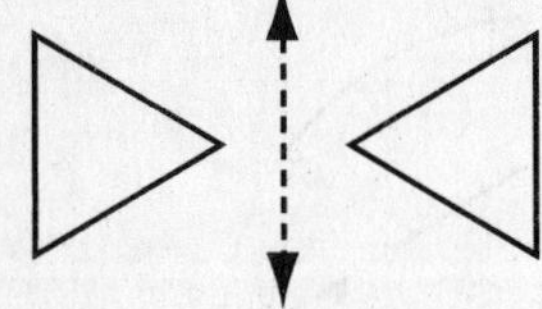

______

2. 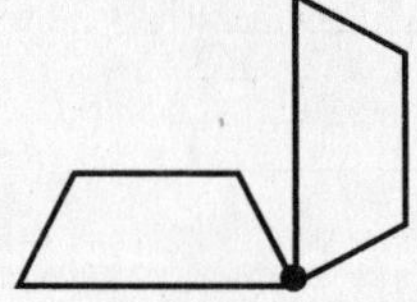

______

3. 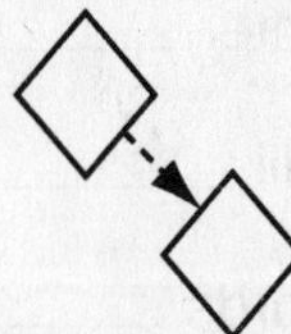

______

4. 

______

5. 

______

6. 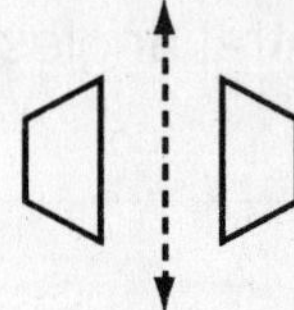

______

Identify the corresponding congruent side or angle.

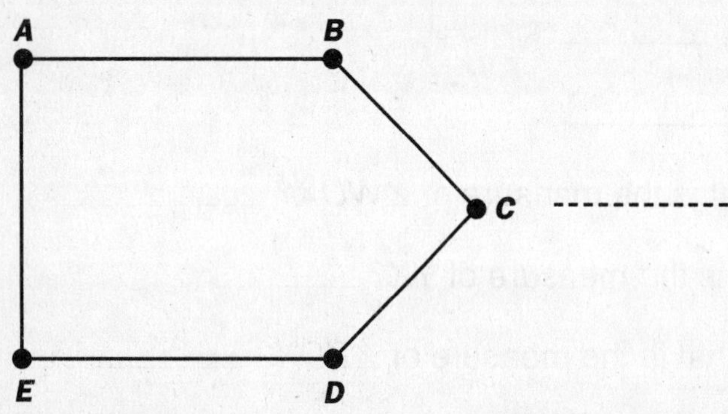

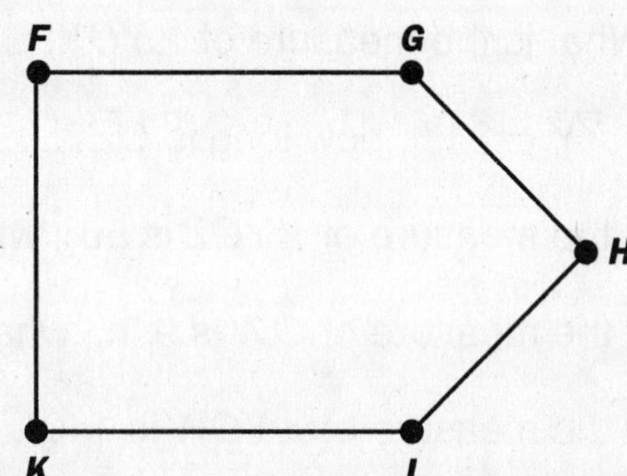

7. $\overline{DE}$ ______

8. $\angle B$ ______

9. $\angle C$ ______

10. $\overline{BC}$ ______

11. $\overline{CD}$ ______

12. $\angle EDC$ ______

Solve.

13. Marcia flips the letter M over the top. What new letter does she make?

______

14. Marcia also flips a square over one of its sides. What figure do the original and flipped squares make together?

______

Name: ______________________

SIMILAR FIGURES

Are the figures similar? Write *yes* or *no.*

1. 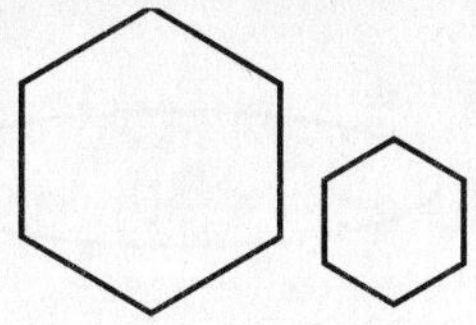
____

2. 
____

3. 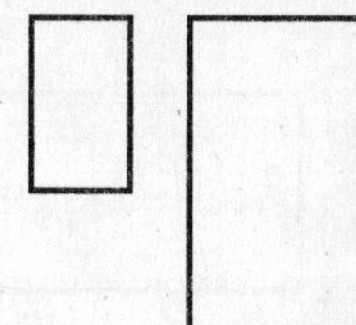
____

4. 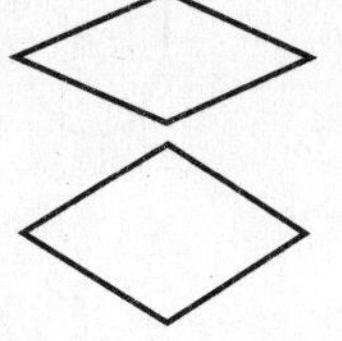
____

5. 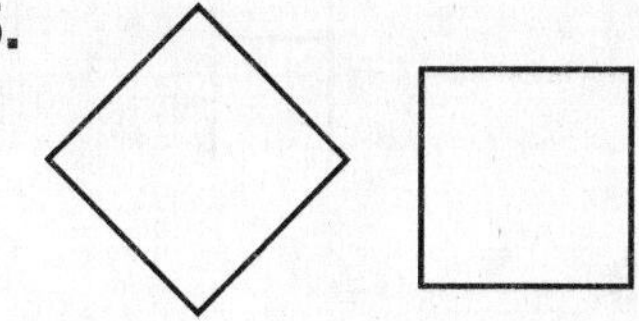
____

6. 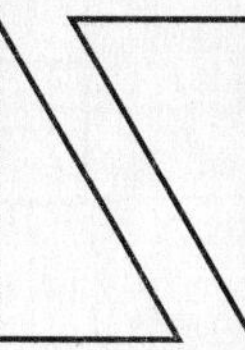
____

7. 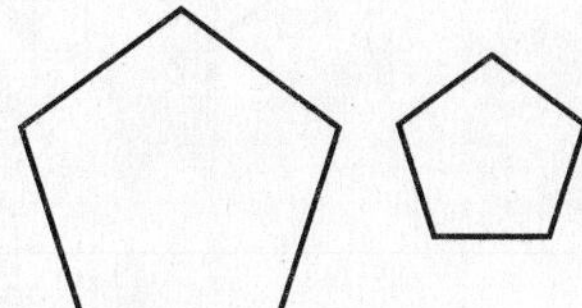
____

8. 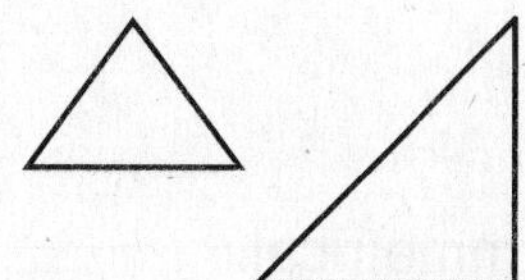
____

9. 
____

Use the grid to draw a figure similar to the given figure.

10. 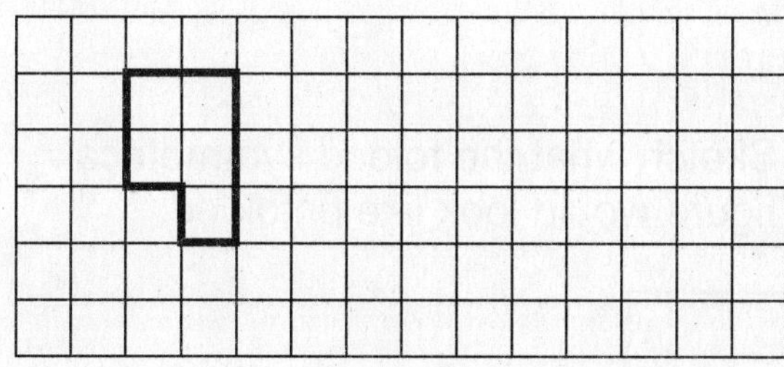

11. 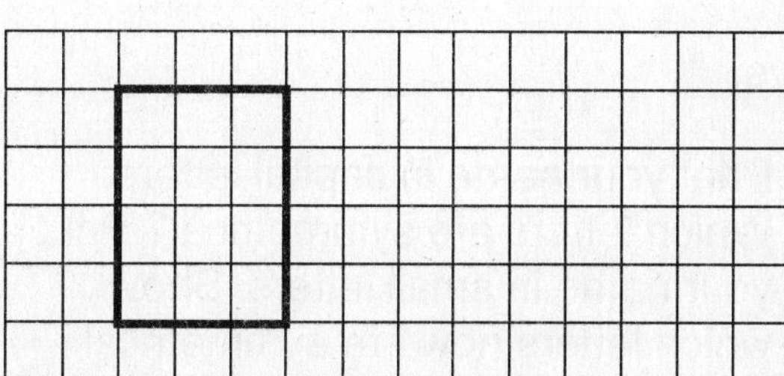

12. 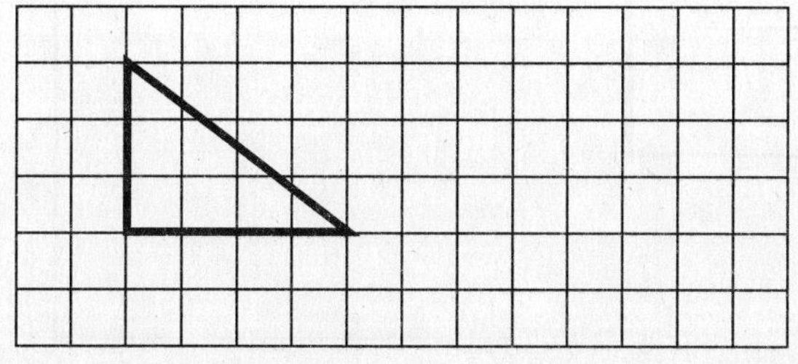

13. 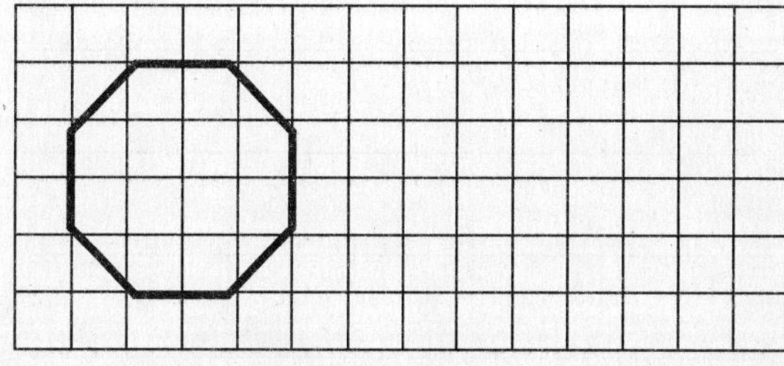

Name:

SYMMETRY

Draw all the lines of symmetry.

1.

2.

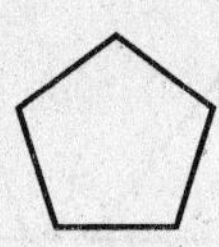

3.

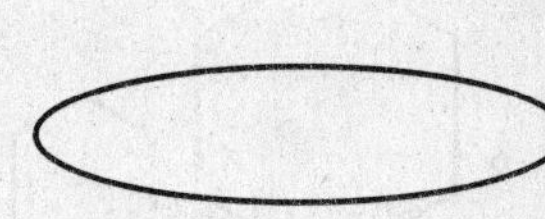

4.

5.

6.

7.

8.

9.

Complete the figure so that it is symmetrical.

10.

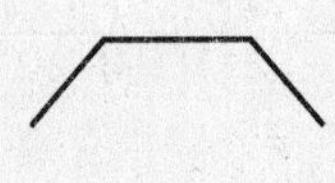

11.

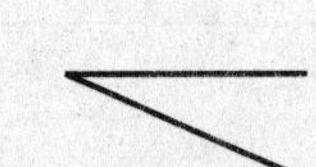

12.

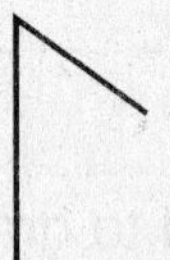

Solve.

13. Print your name in capital letters. Which letters are symmetrical? Print your name in small letters. Show which letters now are symmetrical.

14. Sketch what the folded symmetrical figure would look like unfolded.

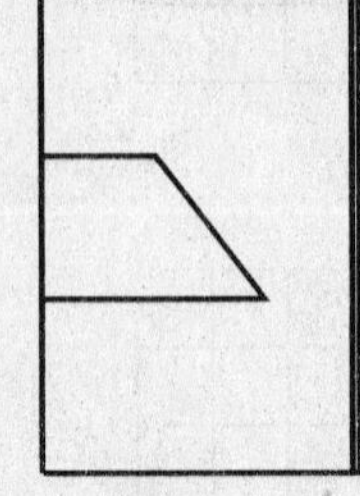

Name:

Coordinate Graphing

Write the ordered pair that names the point in the grid.

1. *R* ________ 2. *S* ________

3. *T* ________ 4. *U* ________

5. *V* ________ 6. *W* ________

7. *X* ________ 8. *Y* ________

9. *Z* ________ 10. *A* ________

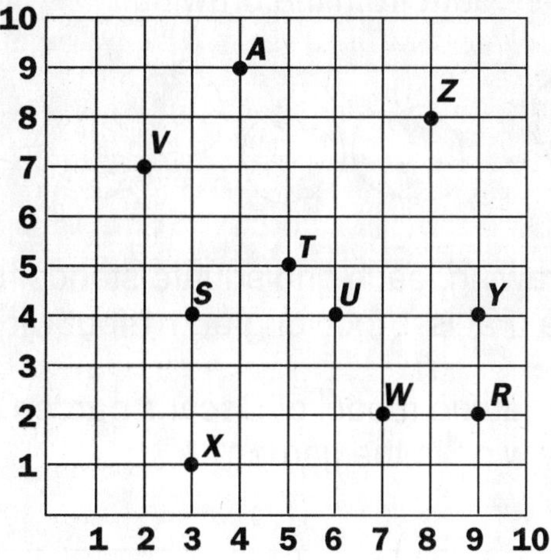

Use the grid below to plot the points. Then connect them in order. Identify the polygon.

11. (4, 2); (10, 2); (10, 5); (4, 5)

____

12. (1, 1); (6, 1); (7, 5); (2, 5)

____

13. (2, 6); (6, 6); (6, 8)

____

14. (3, 3); (4, 7); (7, 7); (8, 3)

____

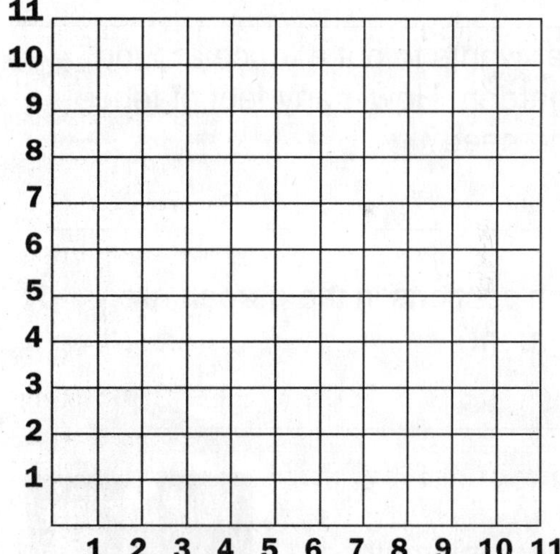

Solve.

15. One point on a line of symmetry of a rectangle is (7, 1). Name another point on the line of symmetry.

____

16. A triangle has vertices of (1, 1), (5, 1), and (3, 4). Name a point on the line of symmetry.

____

Name: ______________________ Practice 78

Problem Solving: Use Data from a Drawing

✔ Read
✔ Plan
✔ Solve
✔ Look Back

Solve. Use data from the drawing.

In the drawing, each grid square stands for a square that is 1 foot long and 1 foot wide.

Herbs
Tomatoes
Lettuce
Beans
Carrots

1. Look at the model of Oscar's garden. How wide is the garden?

____

2. How long is the garden?

____

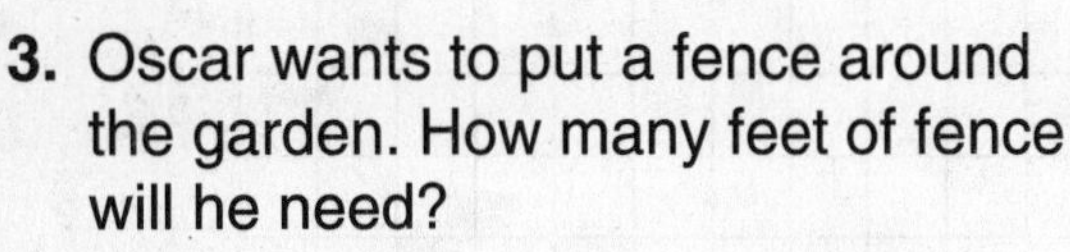

3. Oscar wants to put a fence around the garden. How many feet of fence will he need?

____

4. Suppose Oscar wants to put fencing around each individual garden. Which needs the most? How much does it need?

____

____

5. Which sections in the garden are congruent?

____

Solve using any method.

6. The VGS game system costs $70 less than the Super VGS. The Pretendo system is $110 more than the VGS. The Mega system at $190 is $10 more than the Pretendo. What is the price of each system?

____

____

7. VGS system games cost $55 each. Pretendo system games cost $65 apiece. Denise bought 4 VGS system games. Michael bought 6 Pretendo system games. How much more did Michael spend than Denise?

____

____

Name:

Practice 79

MEANING OF FRACTIONS

Write the fraction for the part that is shaded.

1. 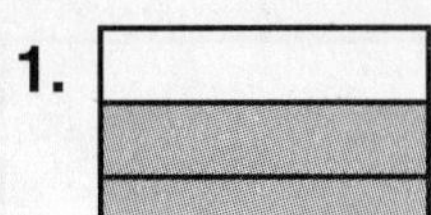 ________

2. ________

3. ________

4. ________

5. ________

6. 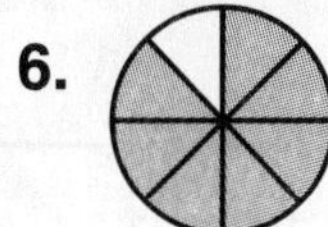 ________

7. 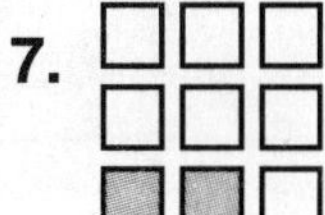 ________

8. 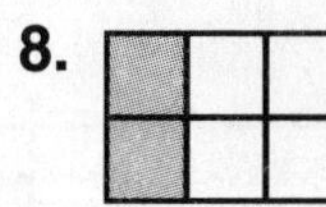 ________

9. ________

10. 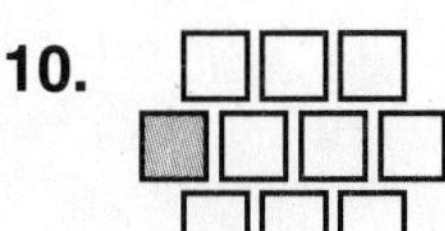 ________

11. 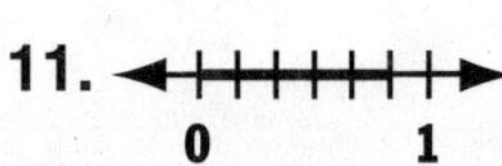

____

12. 0 1 ________

Write the fraction.

13. nine twelfths ________

14. three sixths ________

15. four eighths ________

16. seven eighths ________

17. ten twelfths ________

18. eleven twentieths ________

19. four ninths ________

20. five sixths ________

21. seventeen twentieths ________

22. 0.7 ________

23. 0.1 ________

24. 0.23 ________

25. The numerator is 2.
The denominator is 5. 

26. The numerator is 5.
The denominator is 8. ________

Practice 80

Name: ______________________________

FRACTION BENCHMARKS

Sort the fractions into groups: near 0, near $\frac{1}{2}$, and near 1.

$\frac{1}{7}$	$\frac{4}{15}$	$\frac{8}{9}$	$\frac{7}{10}$	$\frac{3}{7}$	$\frac{4}{10}$
$\frac{1}{8}$	$\frac{6}{9}$	$\frac{1}{6}$	$\frac{5}{8}$	$\frac{4}{5}$	$\frac{6}{7}$
$\frac{4}{7}$	$\frac{3}{8}$	$\frac{9}{10}$	$\frac{2}{12}$	$\frac{8}{10}$	$\frac{3}{5}$
$\frac{2}{9}$	$\frac{5}{6}$	$\frac{2}{5}$	$\frac{7}{9}$	$\frac{7}{8}$	$\frac{6}{10}$

1. Near 0: ______________ **2.** Near $\frac{1}{2}$: ______________ **3.** Near 1: ______________

Is the fraction near 0, $\frac{1}{2}$, or 1?

4. $\frac{11}{20}$ ______________ **5.** $\frac{13}{16}$ ______________ **6.** $\frac{2}{12}$ ______________

7. $\frac{8}{14}$ ______________ **8.** $\frac{12}{30}$ ______________ **9.** $\frac{6}{30}$ ______________

10. $\frac{14}{25}$ ______________ **11.** $\frac{18}{22}$ ______________ **12.** $\frac{2}{15}$ ______________

13. $\frac{20}{100}$ ______________ **14.** $\frac{15}{24}$ ______________ **15.** $\frac{9}{10}$ ______________

16. $\frac{20}{50}$ ______________ **17.** $\frac{1}{3}$ ______________ **18.** $\frac{15}{32}$ ______________

19. $\frac{4}{18}$ ______________ **20.** $\frac{40}{45}$ ______________ **21.** $\frac{16}{30}$ ______________

22. $\frac{3}{18}$ ______________ **23.** $\frac{10}{24}$ ______________ **24.** $\frac{18}{32}$ ______________

25. $\frac{46}{50}$ ______________ **26.** $\frac{90}{100}$ ______________ **27.** $\frac{3}{52}$ ______________

Name: ______________________

Equivalent Fractions

Write two equivalent fractions for the shaded region.

1. 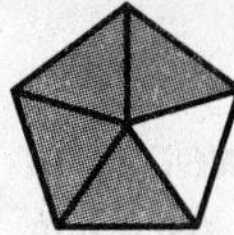

2. 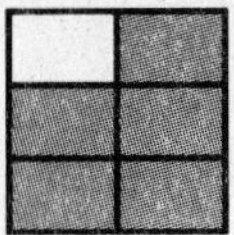

3. 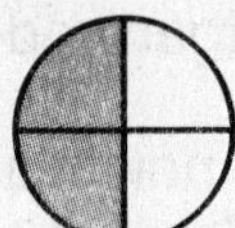

4. 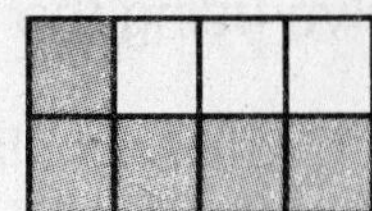

5. 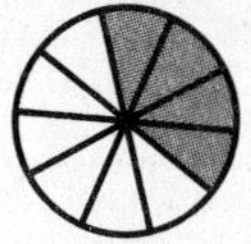

6. 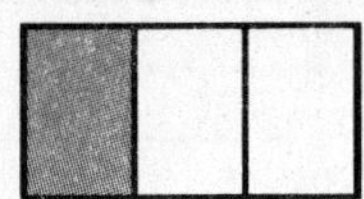

7. 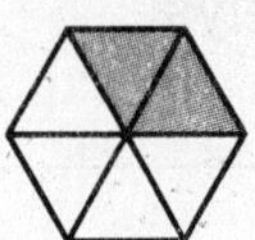

8. 

Complete.

9. $\frac{3}{4} = \frac{9}{\square}$

10. $\frac{12}{20} = \frac{3}{\square}$

11. $\frac{8}{10} = \frac{\square}{5}$

12. $\frac{9}{15} = \frac{3}{\square}$

13. $\frac{10}{20} = \frac{\square}{2}$

14. $\frac{15}{25} = \frac{\square}{5}$

15. $\frac{2}{12} = \frac{1}{\square}$

16. $\frac{6}{9} = \frac{\square}{3}$

17. $\frac{2}{3} = \frac{\square}{18}$

Solve. You may use fraction bars.

18. Elisa walks $\frac{3}{8}$ mile each day to school. Yahira walks $\frac{1}{2}$ mile. Do the girls walk the same distance to school? Explain.

19. Chris completed $\frac{4}{5}$ of his math problems. Anna finished $\frac{20}{25}$. Did they complete the same number of problems? Explain.

Name: ______________________

Problem-Solving Strategy: Make an Organized List

✔ Read
✔ Plan
✔ Solve
✔ Look Back

Solve using the make-an-organized-list strategy.

1. Melissa's class starts a newspaper. It has a trivia column (T), an advice column (A), a review column (R), and a puzzle section (P). How many ways can the newspaper be arranged if the puzzle section is always last? List the ways.

2. In each issue of the newspaper, Melissa's class reviews movies, television shows, music, and books. The order of the reviews depends on the amount of space each review needs. How many different ways can the reviews appear?

3. Jermel pays $2.20 for 20 issues of the newspaper. He pays using two 1-dollar bills and coins. How many ways can he pay for the paper? List them.

4. The students numbered each 4-page issue of the newspaper. The first issue had pages 1–4, the second issue had pages 5–8, the third had 9–12, and so on. As one of the puzzles in the newspaper, Dana asked in which issue the sum of the first and last pages was 45. Which issue was she describing?

Solve using any method.

5. The students pay the cost of producing the newspaper. They plan to sell each copy for $0.15. They will keep enough from the money they earn to cover their expenses. They plan to donate the rest of their money to a charity. If the cost to produce an issue is $4.20 and they sell 50 copies, how much will they donate?

6. The class plans to publish 20 issues during the school year. A student can buy all 20 issues for $2.20 or pay $0.15 for each issue. How much would a student save by paying for all 20 issues at the start of the school year?

Name: ______________________________

Prime and Composite Numbers

Does the model represent a prime number or a composite number?

1. 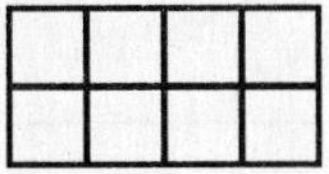

____

2. ______________________

3. 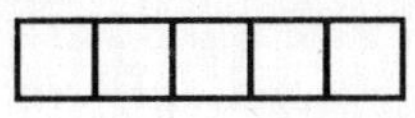

____

4. 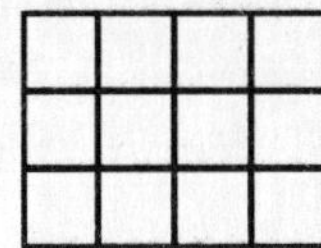

____

List all the factors of the number. Is it *prime* or *composite*?

5. 10 ______________________ **6.** 24 ______________________

7. 23 ______________________ **8.** 26 ______________________

9. 9 ______________________ **10.** 33 ______________________

11. 28 ______________________ **12.** 37 ______________________

13. 42 ______________________ **14.** 38 ______________________

15. 41 ______________________ **16.** 35 ______________________

17. 45 ______________________ **18.** 47 ______________________

19. 40 ______________________ **20.** 34 ______________________

21. 43 ______________________ **22.** 39 ______________________

23. 48 ______________________ **24.** 32 ______________________

Solve.

25. How many prime numbers are less than 30?

____

26. List the prime numbers between 30 and 50.

____

Name: ______________________

GREATEST COMMON FACTOR

List all the factors of the number.

1. 15 ______________________
2. 23 ______________________
3. 17 ______________________
4. 35 ______________________
5. 24 ______________________
6. 33 ______________________
7. 42 ______________________
8. 37 ______________________
9. 28 ______________________
10. 41 ______________________
11. 18 ______________________
12. 32 ______________________

Find the common factors. Then find the GCF.

13. 10 and 22 ______________________
14. 16 and 32 ______________________
15. 12 and 36 ______________________
16. 27 and 30 ______________________
17. 28 and 34 ______________________
18. 18 and 45 ______________________
19. 24 and 30 ______________________
20. 20 and 40 ______________________
21. 14 and 49 ______________________
22. 21 and 45 ______________________
23. 24 and 36 ______________________
24. 21 and 27 ______________________
25. 18 and 16 ______________________
26. 35 and 49 ______________________
27. 8 and 48 ______________________
28. 32 and 40 ______________________
29. 4,12, and 20 ______________________
30. 6, 9, and 24 ______________________
31. 12, 18, and 36 ______________________
32. 9, 15, and 21 ______________________
33. 8, 10, and 24 ______________________
34. 12, 15, and 21 ______________________
35. 18, 24, and 30 ______________________
36. 9, 36, and 45 ______________________

Name: ______________________________

SIMPLIFY FRACTIONS

Complete.

1. $\frac{5}{30} = \frac{\square}{6}$

2. $\frac{4}{28} = \frac{1}{\square}$

3. $\frac{14}{21} = \frac{2}{\square}$

4. $\frac{15}{20} = \frac{3}{\square}$

5. $\frac{16}{18} = \frac{\square}{9}$

6. $\frac{7}{35} = \frac{\square}{5}$

7. $\frac{12}{14} = \frac{6}{\square}$

8. $\frac{3}{30} = \frac{\square}{10}$

9. $\frac{9}{15} = \frac{3}{\square}$

10. $\frac{3}{12} = \frac{1}{\square}$

11. $\frac{4}{32} = \frac{1}{\square}$

12. $\frac{20}{30} = \frac{\square}{3}$

Write in simplest form.

13. $\frac{7}{42}$ ______
14. $\frac{6}{12}$ ______
15. $\frac{4}{16}$ ______
16. $\frac{10}{12}$ ______
17. $\frac{6}{21}$ ______
18. $\frac{5}{25}$ ______
19. $\frac{8}{14}$ ______
20. $\frac{4}{36}$ ______
21. $\frac{10}{30}$ ______
22. $\frac{16}{36}$ ______
23. $\frac{15}{45}$ ______
24. $\frac{20}{25}$ ______
25. $\frac{8}{40}$ ______
26. $\frac{2}{14}$ ______
27. $\frac{30}{35}$ ______
28. $\frac{8}{18}$ ______
29. $\frac{12}{30}$ ______
30. $\frac{9}{24}$ ______
31. $\frac{18}{42}$ ______
32. $\frac{16}{40}$ ______

Solve.

33. Of the 27 students in Jessica's class, 18 receive an allowance each week. What fraction of the students, in simplest form, receives an allowance?

____

34. Of the 18 students who receive an allowance, 16 do chores around the house. What fraction of the students, in simplest form, does chores around the house?

____

Name: ______________________ Practice 86

MIXED NUMBERS

Write as an improper fraction. Do as many as you can mentally.

1. $3\frac{1}{2}$ ________
2. $5\frac{2}{3}$ ________
3. $1\frac{4}{7}$ ________
4. $2\frac{5}{8}$ ________
5. $2\frac{7}{9}$ ________
6. $4\frac{2}{3}$ ________
7. $1\frac{8}{9}$ ________
8. $2\frac{3}{5}$ ________
9. $3\frac{5}{6}$ ________
10. $4\frac{3}{8}$ ________
11. $1\frac{3}{4}$ ________
12. $2\frac{4}{5}$ ________
13. $6\frac{1}{8}$ ________
14. $3\frac{5}{7}$ ________
15. $2\frac{7}{8}$ ________

Write as a whole or mixed number in simplest form.
Do as many as you can mentally.

16. $\frac{30}{3}$ ________
17. $\frac{23}{5}$ ________
18. $\frac{19}{4}$ ________
19. $\frac{43}{6}$ ________
20. $\frac{48}{4}$ ________
21. $\frac{37}{9}$ ________
22. $\frac{25}{8}$ ________
23. $\frac{36}{6}$ ________
24. $\frac{17}{9}$ ________
25. $\frac{32}{7}$ ________
26. $\frac{29}{6}$ ________
27. $\frac{34}{5}$ ________
28. $\frac{31}{4}$ ________
29. $\frac{47}{8}$ ________
30. $\frac{51}{7}$ ________

Solve.

31. The football team shared 30 pizza slices for lunch. There were 2 slices left over. Each pizza was cut into 8 slices. How many pizzas did they eat?

____

32. Another day, the team ate $3\frac{1}{6}$ pizzas for lunch. That day, each slice was $\frac{1}{6}$ of a pizza. How many slices did they eat?

____

Name: ______

Least Common Multiple

Find the LCM.

1. 5 and 15 ______
2. 4 and 6 ______
3. 2 and 11 ______
4. 10 and 15 ______
5. 3 and 8 ______
6. 8 and 12 ______
7. 5 and 7 ______
8. 4 and 8 ______
9. 6 and 9 ______
10. 10 and 25 ______
11. 8 and 9 ______
12. 3 and 5 ______
13. 4 and 5 ______
14. 2 and 9 ______
15. 6 and 15 ______
16. 2 and 3 ______
17. 6 and 7 ______
18. 3 and 4 ______
19. 5 and 12 ______
20. 4 and 14 ______
21. 4 and 10 ______
22. 6 and 10 ______
23. 5 and 8 ______
24. 7 and 8 ______
25. 2, 3, and 4 ______
26. 2, 4, and 16 ______
27. 2, 8, and 10 ______
28. 5, 6, and 12 ______
29. 2, 4, and 9 ______
30. 3, 5, and 6 ______
31. 3, 6, and 8 ______
32. 10, 12, and 15 ______
33. 5, 10, and 15 ______
34. 2, 7, and 14 ______
35. 3, 12, and 16 ______
36. 4, 6, and 15 ______
37. 6, 8, and 16 ______
38. 3, 7, and 14 ______
39. 2, 5, and 10 ______

Solve.

40. Pamela and David begin running laps around the track at the same time. Pamela runs one lap every 8 minutes. David runs a lap every 6 minutes. What is the least amount of time they would both have to run for them to cross the starting line together?

______

41. José and Sara run on the same track. It takes José 9 minutes and Sara 6 minutes to run one lap. If they start running at the same time, how many laps would each have run when they cross the starting line together for the first time?

______

Name: ______________________ **Practice 88**

Compare and Order Fractions and Mixed Numbers

Write in order from least to greatest.

1. $\frac{1}{5}, \frac{1}{6}, \frac{5}{10}$ ______

2. $\frac{3}{4}, \frac{2}{8}, \frac{1}{3}$ ______

3. $\frac{5}{8}, \frac{1}{2}, \frac{2}{5}$ ______

4. $\frac{9}{10}, \frac{4}{5}, \frac{2}{3}$ ______

5. $\frac{2}{3}, \frac{1}{6}, \frac{2}{5}$ ______

6. $\frac{5}{6}, \frac{3}{10}, \frac{1}{2}$ ______

7. $\frac{1}{5}, \frac{1}{8}, \frac{3}{6}$ ______

8. $1\frac{3}{4}, 1\frac{4}{5}, 2$ ______

9. $2\frac{3}{8}, 2\frac{2}{5}, 2$ ______

10. $3\frac{2}{3}, 3\frac{5}{8}, 3$ ______

11. $1\frac{9}{10}, 1\frac{2}{3}, 1\frac{3}{4}$ ______

12. $2, 1\frac{8}{10}, 1\frac{5}{6}$ ______

Write in order from greatest to least.

13. $\frac{3}{4}, \frac{1}{2}, \frac{5}{6}$ ______

14. $\frac{1}{4}, \frac{5}{8}, \frac{6}{10}$ ______

15. $\frac{5}{8}, \frac{5}{9}, \frac{2}{3}$ ______

16. $\frac{5}{8}, \frac{9}{10}, \frac{3}{4}$ ______

17. $\frac{7}{8}, \frac{2}{3}, \frac{9}{12}$ ______

18. $\frac{3}{8}, \frac{5}{10}, \frac{2}{5}$ ______

19. $\frac{1}{3}, \frac{1}{8}, \frac{2}{5}$ ______

20. $1\frac{2}{3}, 1\frac{5}{7}, 1$ ______

21. $2\frac{2}{3}, 2\frac{4}{5}, 2$ ______

22. $4\frac{5}{6}, 4\frac{5}{7}, 5$ ______

Solve.

23. Shawn said he spent $1\frac{2}{3}$ hours on his homework. Carol said hers took longer—$1\frac{1}{2}$ hours. Was Carol correct? How do you know?

______

24. Dennis took $\frac{3}{4}$ of the allowed time to complete his math test. Sharlene used $\frac{2}{3}$ of the time and Paul used $\frac{5}{6}$ of the time. Write the students in the order of the amount of time they used, from least to greatest.

______

Name: ______________________________

Compare Whole Numbers, Mixed Numbers, and Decimals

Compare. Write >, <, or =.

1. $\frac{3}{4}$ ◯ 0.9 **2.** 0.5 ◯ $\frac{1}{5}$ **3.** 0.3 ◯ $\frac{5}{6}$

4. 0.9 ◯ $\frac{9}{4}$ **5.** $\frac{9}{4}$ ◯ 2.4 **6.** $\frac{3}{4}$ ◯ 0.6

7. 3.7 ◯ $\frac{3}{7}$ **8.** $\frac{9}{2}$ ◯ 9.1 **9.** 0.4 ◯ $\frac{1}{4}$

10. $\frac{1}{5}$ ◯ 0.5 **11.** 0.75 ◯ $\frac{3}{4}$ **12.** 0.6 ◯ $\frac{3}{4}$

13. 0.25 ◯ $\frac{2}{5}$ **14.** $\frac{9}{2}$ ◯ 9.2 **15.** 0.55 ◯ $\frac{1}{2}$

16. $\frac{2}{3}$ ◯ $2\frac{1}{3}$ **17.** 0.3 ◯ $\frac{3}{2}$ **18.** $2\frac{3}{5}$ ◯ 2.6

Write in order from least to greatest.

19. $\frac{6}{10}$, 0.5, $\frac{1}{3}$ ______________

20. $\frac{1}{2}$, 0.4, $\frac{3}{4}$ ______________

21. $\frac{9}{10}$, 0.8, $\frac{3}{5}$ ______________

22. 0.2, 0.9, $\frac{3}{5}$ ______________

23. 0.6, 5.6, $5\frac{3}{6}$ ______________

24. 0.8, $\frac{5}{8}$, 2 ______________

25. $\frac{4}{2}$, 4, $\frac{2}{4}$ ______________

26. 4.2, 4, $4\frac{1}{4}$ ______________

27. 0.85, 0.65, $\frac{3}{4}$ ______________

28. 6, $5\frac{1}{3}$, 5.28 ______________

Solve.

29. Martin entered a footrace that covered $6\frac{2}{5}$ miles. If Martin runs 6.2 miles, does he finish the race? How do you know?

____

30. Rita tried to break the school high-jump record of $5\frac{3}{4}$ feet. On her best jump she cleared 5.5 feet. Did she succeed? Explain your answer.

____

Name: ______________________ **Practice 90**

PROBLEM SOLVING: SOLVE MULTISTEP PROBLEMS

✔ Read
✔ Plan
✔ Solve
✔ Look Back

Use the table to solve problems 1–3.

CALORIES BURNED PER HOUR	
Activity	**Calories**
Running (6 mph)	about 570
Soccer	about 455
Tennis	about 380
Cycling	about 360
Walking (2 mph)	about 160

1. John plays 2 hours of soccer and 3 hours of tennis every week. What is the average number of calories he burns per day?

____

2. Tony planned to exercise enough to burn an average of 500 extra calories a day. This week he ran for 2 hours, walked for 6 hours, and cycled for 5 hours. Did he meet his goal? By how many calories was he over or under his goal?

____

____

3. Eight members of the tennis team played tennis for 2 hours each day for 5 days. How many calories did the team burn altogether from this activity?

____

Solve using any method.

4. At the Red Rose Music Store, song books cost \$12.95. Individual sheet music is \$1.79. How much less will it cost to buy a song book than a dozen pieces of sheet music?

____

5. During a music sale you can buy 2 CDs for the price of 1. If a CD sells for \$9.95 and tapes are \$2.49, how much will you pay for 6 CDs and 3 tapes?

____

6. Mrs. Viola charges \$15.00 for a 1-hour piano lesson. She gives her students 1 free lesson for every 6 lessons they take. How much will you pay her for 28 lessons?

____

7. Max bought 2 CDs at \$8.49 each, 3 tapes at \$3.50 each, and a CD case for \$13.00. He gave the clerk \$50.00. How much change did he get back?

____

Name: ____________________

ADD FRACTIONS

Add. You may use a model to help you.

1. $\frac{2}{5} + \frac{1}{5}$

2. $\frac{3}{8} + \frac{2}{8}$

3. $\frac{7}{10} + \frac{2}{10}$

4. $\frac{3}{6} + \frac{2}{6}$

5. $\frac{1}{7} + \frac{2}{7}$

6. $\frac{3}{10} + \frac{4}{10}$

7. $\frac{5}{6} + \frac{1}{6}$

8. $\frac{1}{6} + \frac{2}{3}$

9. $\frac{1}{9} + \frac{2}{9}$

10. $\frac{1}{8} + \frac{1}{8}$

11. $\frac{5}{8} + \frac{1}{4}$

12. $\frac{3}{5} + \frac{1}{10}$

13. $\frac{1}{6} + \frac{1}{3}$

14. $\frac{1}{3} + \frac{1}{2}$

15. $\frac{1}{10} + \frac{4}{5}$

16. $\frac{1}{3} + \frac{1}{12}$

17. $\frac{3}{8} + \frac{2}{4}$

18. $\frac{5}{7} + \frac{3}{14}$

19. $\frac{3}{10} + \frac{1}{5}$

20. $\frac{1}{8} + \frac{3}{4}$

21. $\frac{1}{2} + \frac{1}{10}$

22. $\frac{5}{9} + \frac{1}{3}$

23. $\frac{1}{12} + \frac{3}{4}$

24. $\frac{1}{4} + \frac{2}{3}$

25. $\frac{1}{3} + \frac{1}{4}$

26. $\frac{1}{2} + \frac{1}{8} =$ ____________

27. $\frac{3}{10} + \frac{1}{5} =$ ____________

28. $\frac{2}{8} + \frac{3}{4} =$ ____________

29. $\frac{1}{5} + \frac{1}{10} =$ ____________

30. $\frac{1}{4} + \frac{1}{6} =$ ____________

31. $\frac{2}{6} + \frac{1}{3} =$ ____________

32. $\frac{2}{12} + \frac{1}{4} =$ ____________

33. $\frac{2}{3} + \frac{1}{12} =$ ____________

34. $\frac{1}{4} + \frac{1}{8} =$ ____________

Name:

Add Fractions

Add. Write the answer in simplest form.

1. $\frac{1}{4} + \frac{2}{4}$

2. $\frac{2}{5} + \frac{2}{5}$

3. $\frac{5}{8} + \frac{1}{8}$

4. $\frac{7}{12} + \frac{4}{12}$

5. $\frac{7}{15} + \frac{3}{15}$

6. $\frac{1}{3} + \frac{1}{6}$

7. $\frac{2}{9} + \frac{1}{3}$

8. $\frac{3}{5} + \frac{1}{10}$

9. $\frac{5}{12} + \frac{2}{6}$

10. $\frac{3}{4} + \frac{5}{12}$

11. $\frac{1}{5} + \frac{1}{2} =$ ________

12. $\frac{1}{8} + \frac{5}{6} =$ ________

13. $\frac{5}{8} + \frac{1}{3} =$ ________

14. $\frac{1}{3} + \frac{1}{4} + \frac{1}{12} =$ ______

15. $\frac{1}{8} + \frac{3}{8} + \frac{1}{4} =$ ______

16. $\frac{1}{3} + \frac{7}{12} + \frac{1}{24} =$ ______

Algebra Complete the table. Write the output in simplest form.

17.

Rule: Add $\frac{1}{4}$	
Input	**Output**
$\frac{3}{8}$	
$\frac{1}{4}$	
$\frac{1}{3}$	
$\frac{1}{2}$	

18.

Rule: Add $\frac{1}{9}$	
Input	**Output**
$\frac{1}{6}$	
$\frac{2}{9}$	
$\frac{1}{3}$	
$\frac{5}{6}$	

19.

Rule: Add $\frac{1}{10}$	
Input	**Output**
$\frac{1}{5}$	
$\frac{3}{10}$	
$\frac{1}{2}$	
$\frac{3}{5}$	

Name:

Practice 93

SUBTRACT FRACTIONS

Subtract. You may use a model to help you.

1. $\frac{5}{6} - \frac{4}{6}$

2. $\frac{11}{12} - \frac{4}{12}$

3. $\frac{4}{7} - \frac{3}{7}$

4. $\frac{6}{9} - \frac{2}{9}$

5. $\frac{7}{8} - \frac{4}{8}$

6. $\frac{9}{10} - \frac{4}{10}$

7. $\frac{3}{4} - \frac{1}{4}$

8. $\frac{7}{8} - \frac{5}{8}$

9. $\frac{5}{8} - \frac{1}{4}$

10. $\frac{7}{10} - \frac{1}{2}$

11. $\frac{2}{3} - \frac{1}{2}$

12. $\frac{2}{5} - \frac{1}{10}$

13. $\frac{5}{8} - \frac{2}{4}$

14. $\frac{5}{6} - \frac{1}{3}$

15. $\frac{3}{4} - \frac{1}{3}$

16. $\frac{4}{5} - \frac{1}{2}$

17. $\frac{9}{12} - \frac{2}{3}$

18. $\frac{7}{8} - \frac{1}{4}$

19. $\frac{7}{8} - \frac{1}{2}$

20. $\frac{2}{3} - \frac{1}{6}$

21. $\frac{7}{10} - \frac{2}{5}$

22. $\frac{5}{6} - \frac{1}{4}$

23. $\frac{5}{6} - \frac{1}{12}$

24. $\frac{7}{9} - \frac{1}{3}$

25. $\frac{3}{10} - \frac{1}{5}$

26. $\frac{5}{9} - \frac{1}{3} =$ ________

27. $\frac{9}{10} - \frac{4}{5} =$ ________

28. $\frac{3}{4} - \frac{3}{8} =$ ________

29. $\frac{3}{4} - \frac{1}{8} =$ ________

30. $\frac{5}{6} - \frac{1}{2} =$ ________

31. $\frac{2}{3} - \frac{1}{4} =$ ________

32. $\frac{7}{8} - \frac{3}{4} =$ ________

33. $\frac{5}{6} - \frac{2}{3} =$ ________

34. $\frac{3}{5} - \frac{1}{2} =$ ________

Name: **Practice 94**

SUBTRACT FRACTIONS

Subtract. Write the answer in simplest form.

1. $\frac{7}{8} - \frac{1}{8}$

2. $\frac{5}{6} - \frac{1}{6}$

3. $\frac{3}{4} - \frac{1}{4}$

4. $\frac{11}{12} - \frac{7}{12}$

5. $\frac{7}{12} - \frac{5}{12}$

6. $\frac{5}{8} - \frac{3}{8}$

7. $\frac{4}{5} - \frac{2}{5}$

8. $\frac{9}{10} - \frac{3}{10}$

9. $\frac{7}{9} - \frac{2}{3}$

10. $\frac{7}{8} - \frac{1}{4}$

11. $\frac{2}{3} - \frac{1}{2} =$ ______

12. $\frac{5}{6} - \frac{3}{4} =$ ______

13. $\frac{3}{4} - \frac{2}{3} =$ ______

14. $\frac{5}{6} - \frac{1}{4} =$ ______

15. $\frac{7}{12} - \frac{3}{8} =$ ______

16. $\frac{11}{12} - \frac{1}{2} =$ ______

Algebra Complete the table. Write the output in simplest form.

17.

Rule: Subtract $\frac{1}{4}$	
Input	**Output**
$\frac{7}{8}$	
$\frac{3}{4}$	
$\frac{1}{2}$	
$\frac{5}{8}$	

18.

Rule: Subtract $\frac{1}{6}$	
Input	**Output**
$\frac{1}{2}$	
$\frac{5}{6}$	
$\frac{2}{3}$	
$\frac{7}{12}$	

19.

Rule: Subtract $\frac{1}{10}$	
Input	**Output**
$\frac{2}{5}$	
$\frac{9}{10}$	
$\frac{1}{2}$	
$\frac{3}{4}$	

Name:

Problem-Solving Strategy: Work Backward

✔ Read
✔ Plan
✔ Solve
✔ Look Back

Solve using the work-backward strategy.

1. Amanda, Sarah, and Laurie compared how much they spent on pet food for the year. Laurie spent $50 less for her hamster than Sarah spent for her guinea pig. Amanda spent 5 times as much for her Great Dane as Sarah spent. If Amanda spent $400, how much did each of the other girls spend?

2. Jackson works in the pet store. He spends 2 hours feeding the animals and $1\frac{1}{2}$ hours cleaning their cages. It takes him 1 hour to stock the shelves and $\frac{1}{2}$ hour to clean the filters in the fish tanks. If he wants to go home at 6 P.M., at what time should he start his chores?

3. Denise spends about 6 times longer taking care of her dog each week than Kerry spends taking care of her goldfish. Jamie spends half as much time on her cat as Denise does for her dog. Kerry spends 30 minutes taking care of her goldfish each week. How long do Denise and Jamie spend on their pets?

4. Andy is making plastic collars for his 3 dogs. He uses 2 inches less plastic for his terrier than for his beagle. He uses 6 inches more plastic for his collie than for his beagle. If he uses 18 inches of plastic for his collie, how many inches of plastic does he use in all?

Solve using any method.

5. **Logical Reasoning** Rhonda, Sally, and Thomas own a cat, a dog, and a hamster, but not necessarily in that order. Rhonda does not own a cat or a hamster. Thomas does not own a hamster. Who owns each pet?

6. A kennel has sections that can house no more than 8 dogs each. If there are 58 dogs in the kennel, how many sections are in use? How many of the sections are full?

Name: ____________

Practice 96

ESTIMATE WITH MIXED NUMBERS

Estimate the sum or difference.

1. $1\frac{7}{8} + 1\frac{1}{6}$ ______ **2.** $2\frac{1}{3} - 1\frac{1}{5}$ ______ **3.** $2\frac{5}{6} - 1\frac{2}{3}$ ______

4. $3\frac{1}{4} + 2\frac{1}{2}$ ______ **5.** $5\frac{7}{10} + 2\frac{4}{5}$ ______ **6.** $4\frac{1}{8} + 3\frac{2}{9}$ ______

7. $6\frac{5}{6} - 3\frac{2}{3}$ ______ **8.** $8\frac{3}{10} - 4\frac{7}{8}$ ______ **9.** $9 - 6\frac{2}{3}$ ______

10. $5\frac{5}{6} - 2$ ______ **11.** $10\frac{6}{7} - 3\frac{1}{3}$ ______ **12.** $7 + 6\frac{9}{10}$ ______

13. $4 - 2\frac{7}{8}$ ______ **14.** $3\frac{2}{3} + 4\frac{2}{3}$ ______ **15.** $5\frac{2}{3} + 6\frac{7}{8}$ ______

16. $9\frac{1}{2} - 5\frac{3}{4}$ ______ **17.** $21\frac{1}{5} + 11\frac{1}{4}$ ______ **18.** $19 - 7\frac{7}{8}$ ______

19. $49\frac{4}{5} - 28\frac{7}{8}$ ______ **20.** $17 + 6\frac{9}{10}$ ______ **21.** $58\frac{1}{3} + 28\frac{3}{4}$ ______

Estimate to compare. Write >, <, or =.

22. $2\frac{5}{6} + 3\frac{7}{8}$ ◯ 8 **23.** $4\frac{3}{4} - 1\frac{9}{10}$ ◯ 2 **24.** $4\frac{7}{8} + 6\frac{7}{8}$ ◯ 11

25. $6\frac{3}{8} + 3\frac{9}{10}$ ◯ 9 **26.** $12 - 5\frac{1}{3}$ ◯ 7 **27.** $16 - 4\frac{5}{6}$ ◯ 11

Solve.

28. Rosa wanted to walk at least 8 miles by the end of the week. She walked a total of $5\frac{3}{4}$ miles by Thursday. If she walks another $2\frac{1}{2}$ miles on Friday, will she meet her goal? How do you know?

______

29. After walking $10\frac{7}{8}$ miles one week, Rosa walked about $2\frac{1}{2}$ fewer miles the following week. About how many miles did she walk the second week?

______

Name:

ADD MIXED NUMBERS

Add. You may use a model to help you.

1. $1\frac{1}{3} + 2\frac{2}{3}$

2. $2\frac{5}{8} + 1\frac{3}{8}$

3. $7\frac{1}{4} + 2\frac{3}{4}$

4. $2\frac{2}{5} + 4\frac{2}{5}$

5. $4\frac{1}{4} + 1\frac{1}{8}$

6. $2\frac{7}{10} + 4\frac{1}{5}$

7. $3\frac{1}{2} + 5\frac{1}{4}$

8. $1\frac{1}{8} + 3\frac{3}{4}$

9. $2\frac{3}{5} + 3\frac{7}{10}$

10. $6\frac{5}{8} + \frac{3}{4}$

11. $\frac{3}{4} + 4\frac{3}{8}$

12. $\frac{9}{10} + 7\frac{3}{5}$

13. $5\frac{1}{5} + 2\frac{1}{10}$

14. $7\frac{7}{8} + \frac{7}{8}$

15. $3\frac{1}{2} + 2\frac{5}{6}$

16. $1\frac{3}{5} + \frac{3}{5}$

17. $1\frac{1}{6} + 3\frac{2}{3} =$ ________

18. $3\frac{1}{3} + 2\frac{1}{4} =$ ________

19. $2\frac{5}{8} + 2\frac{5}{8} =$ ________

20. $4\frac{1}{2} + 3\frac{1}{5} =$ ________

21. $3\frac{4}{5} + 3\frac{4}{5} =$ ________

22. $1\frac{2}{3} + 2\frac{1}{4} =$ ________

23. $2\frac{1}{2} + 3\frac{4}{5} =$ ________

24. $3\frac{3}{4} + 2\frac{2}{3} =$ ________

25. $1\frac{7}{8} + \frac{3}{4} =$ ________

26. $4\frac{2}{3} + 5\frac{5}{6} =$ ________

27. $2\frac{3}{5} + 6\frac{3}{10} =$ ________

28. $2\frac{3}{8} + 5\frac{1}{4} =$ ________

Name: ____________ **Practice 98**

SUBTRACT MIXED NUMBERS

Do you need to rename a mixed number to find the difference? Write *yes* or *no*.

1. $6\frac{1}{3} - 3\frac{5}{6}$ ______
2. $4\frac{3}{4} - 2\frac{1}{2}$ ______
3. $5\frac{3}{8} - 2\frac{1}{2}$ ______
4. $6\frac{3}{8} - 4\frac{7}{8}$ ______
5. $8\frac{5}{6} - 4$ ______
6. $3\frac{1}{3} - 1\frac{1}{6}$ ______
7. $7\frac{1}{4} - 5\frac{3}{8}$ ______
8. $5\frac{3}{4} - 2\frac{1}{2}$ ______
9. $4\frac{7}{9} - 3\frac{2}{3}$ ______
10. $5\frac{1}{3} - 2\frac{3}{4}$ ______
11. $3\frac{3}{8} - 1\frac{1}{2}$ ______
12. $7\frac{1}{3} - 2\frac{2}{9}$ ______

Subtract. You may use a model to help you.

13. $3\frac{2}{3} - 1\frac{1}{3}$
14. $5\frac{3}{4} - 3\frac{1}{4}$
15. $3\frac{5}{6} - \frac{1}{6}$
16. $8\frac{5}{9} - 5\frac{2}{9}$
17. $2\frac{1}{4} - \frac{3}{4}$
18. $3\frac{3}{8} - 1\frac{5}{8}$
19. $1 - \frac{3}{8}$
20. $4\frac{3}{5} - 1\frac{4}{5}$
21. $4\frac{1}{2} - 1\frac{3}{4}$
22. $2\frac{3}{8} - \frac{3}{4}$
23. $6\frac{3}{5} - 3\frac{9}{10}$
24. $5\frac{3}{8} - 2\frac{1}{2}$
25. $4\frac{2}{3} - 2\frac{5}{6} =$ ______
26. $4\frac{1}{6} - 1\frac{1}{2} =$ ______
27. $7\frac{5}{12} - 2\frac{1}{3} =$ ______
28. $1\frac{3}{5} - \frac{3}{10} =$ ______
29. $5 - 2\frac{3}{4} =$ ______
30. $8 - 6\frac{2}{5} =$ ______
31. $4\frac{1}{3} - 1\frac{5}{6} =$ ______
32. $7\frac{3}{4} - 3\frac{5}{8} =$ ______
33. $6\frac{1}{4} - 4\frac{7}{8} =$ ______
34. $5 - 3\frac{7}{10} =$ ______
35. $4\frac{1}{2} - 1\frac{9}{10} =$ ______
36. $8\frac{1}{2} - \frac{5}{8} =$ ______

Name: ______

Add and Subtract Mixed Numbers

Add. Write the answer in simplest form. Remember to estimate.

1. $1\frac{1}{5} + 2\frac{3}{5}$

2. $3\frac{1}{8} + 4\frac{5}{8}$

3. $2\frac{5}{8} + 5\frac{3}{8}$

4. $2\frac{1}{4} + 1\frac{1}{2}$

5. $2\frac{7}{8} + 5\frac{3}{8}$

6. $3\frac{1}{2} + \frac{3}{4}$

7. $6\frac{2}{3} + 1\frac{1}{4}$

8. $4\frac{3}{5} + 4\frac{7}{10}$

9. $2 + 1\frac{7}{8} + 3\frac{3}{4} =$ ______

10. $3\frac{4}{9} + 2\frac{2}{3} + 2 =$ ______

11. $6\frac{2}{3} + 4 + 3\frac{5}{6} =$ ______

Subtract. Write the answer in simplest form. Remember to estimate.

12. $2\frac{5}{8} - 1\frac{3}{8}$

13. $3\frac{3}{4} - 1\frac{1}{2}$

14. $8\frac{1}{2} - 5\frac{1}{3}$

15. $6 - 3\frac{4}{5}$

16. $4 - 1\frac{3}{8}$

17. $3\frac{3}{10} - \frac{1}{2}$

18. $4\frac{5}{6} - 1\frac{1}{3}$

19. $9\frac{1}{8} - 7\frac{3}{4}$

20. $7\frac{1}{2} - 3\frac{5}{8} =$ ______

21. $3\frac{4}{9} - 2\frac{1}{3} =$ ______

22. $3\frac{11}{12} - 1\frac{2}{3} =$ ______

Name: ______________________________

Problem Solving: Use a Diagram

✔ Read
✔ Plan
✔ Solve
✔ Look Back

Solve using the use-a-diagram strategy. Use the grid for problems 1–3.

1. The streets of a town are arranged in a square grid. There are 8 streets running west to east and 8 streets running south to north. How many square blocks are there in the town? Complete the diagram to help solve the problem.

   ____

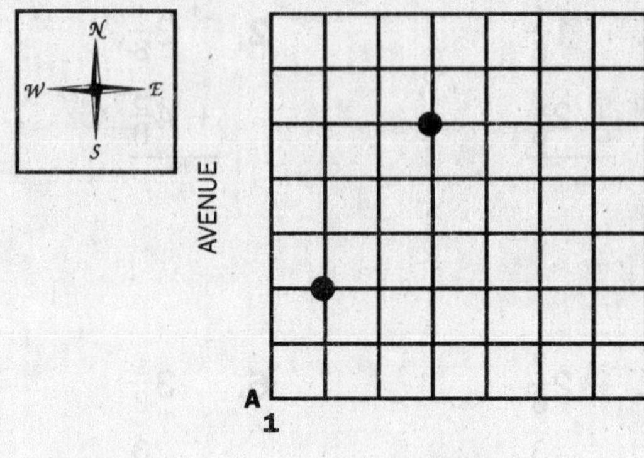

2. From west to east the streets are numbered from First Street to Eighth Street. From south to north the streets use letters from Avenue A to Avenue H. Audrey lives on the corner of Third Street and Avenue C. What is the shortest walking distance from her home to the home of her friend Carla, who lives on the corner of Fifth Street and Avenue F?

   ____

   ____

3. Audrey likes to take different routes when she visits Carla. If she only walks north or east, what are the different routes from her house to Carla's? Use the diagram above to make an organized list.

   ____

   ____

   ____

   ____

Pencil & Paper 

Solve using any method.

4. Each block in town is 300 feet long. How far is it from Audrey's home to Carla's home?

   ____

   ____

   ____

5. Audrey likes to give her address in the form of a riddle. She tells new friends that her address is a number less than 100 that has exactly 10 factors. The sum of the digits of the number is 12. What is the number of Audrey's address?

   ____

Name: ______________________

FIND A FRACTION OF A WHOLE NUMBER

Write a multiplication sentence for each diagram.

1. 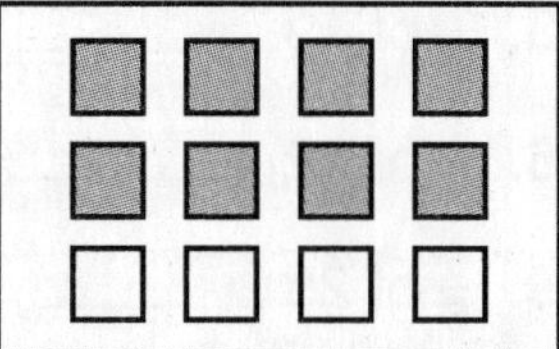
____

2. 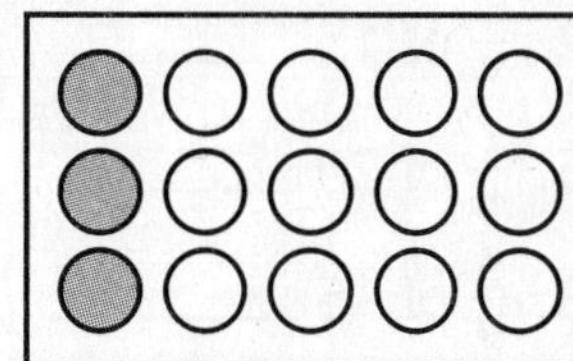
____

3. 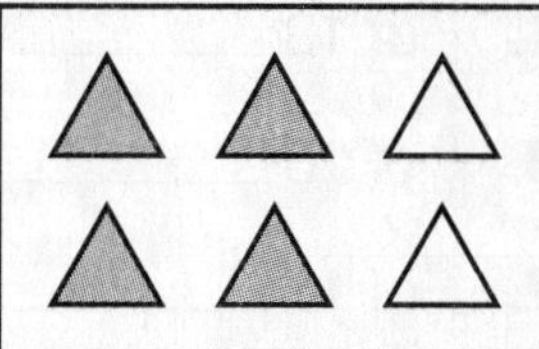
____

4. 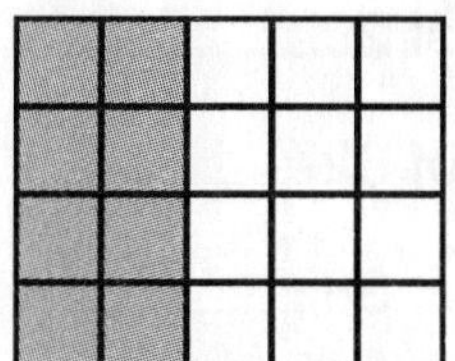
____

5. 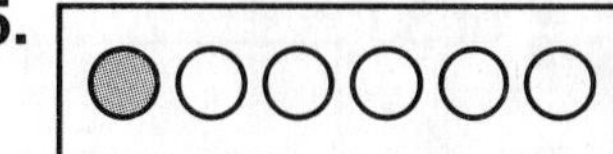
____

6. 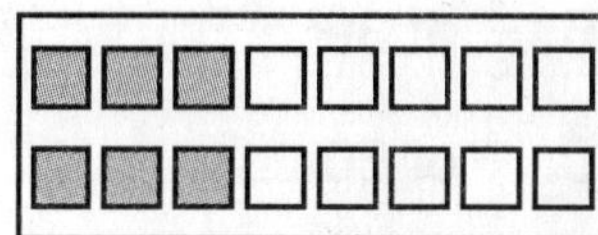
____

Solve.

7. $\frac{1}{3}$ of 12 ________
8. $\frac{1}{9}$ of 18 ________
9. $\frac{1}{4}$ of 16 ________
10. $\frac{1}{3}$ of 30 ________
11. $\frac{1}{7}$ of 14 ________
12. $\frac{1}{5}$ of 5 ________
13. $\frac{2}{5}$ of 15 ________
14. $\frac{4}{5}$ of 15 ________
15. $\frac{5}{6}$ of 12 ________
16. $\frac{7}{8}$ of 24 ________
17. $\frac{3}{8}$ of 24 ________
18. $\frac{2}{5}$ of 25 ________
19. $\frac{2}{3}$ of 24 ________
20. $\frac{5}{6}$ of 6 ________
21. $\frac{2}{9}$ of 18 ________
22. $25 \times \frac{3}{5}$ ________
23. $24 \times \frac{5}{6}$ ________
24. $\frac{9}{10} \times 20$ ________
25. $\frac{6}{7} \times 14$ ________
26. $\frac{3}{8} \times 16$ ________
27. $\frac{5}{6} \times 30$ ________
28. $\frac{4}{5} \times 25$ ________
29. $\frac{3}{4} \times 8$ ________
30. $\frac{2}{3} \times 12$ ________
31. $\frac{2}{7}$ of 28 ________
32. $\frac{1}{3}$ of 45 ________
33. $\frac{1}{4}$ of 28 ________
34. $\frac{4}{9}$ of 63 ________
35. $\frac{2}{3}$ of 36 ________
36. $\frac{4}{5}$ of 35 ________
37. $\frac{9}{10}$ of 80 ________
38. $\frac{3}{7}$ of 42 ________
39. $\frac{5}{8}$ of 64 ________

Name: ________________________________

Mental Math: Estimate a Fraction of a Number

Estimate. Do as many as you can mentally.

1. $\frac{1}{2}$ of 13 ______
2. $\frac{1}{4}$ of 15 ______
3. $\frac{1}{3}$ of 19 ______
4. $\frac{1}{8}$ of 26 ______
5. $\frac{1}{6}$ of 29 ______
6. $\frac{1}{8}$ of 22 ______
7. $\frac{2}{5}$ of 17 ______
8. $\frac{3}{4}$ of 15 ______
9. $\frac{5}{6}$ of 25 ______
10. $20 \times \frac{1}{7}$ ______
11. $\frac{2}{3}$ of 29 ______
12. $\frac{3}{5}$ of 32 ______
13. $34 \times \frac{1}{6}$ ______
14. $\frac{2}{7}$ of 15 ______
15. $\frac{5}{12}$ of 37 ______
16. $\frac{4}{5}$ of 39 ______
17. $\frac{3}{8}$ of 33 ______
18. $\frac{2}{5}$ of 28 ______
19. $\frac{3}{4}$ of 50 ______
20. $44 \times \frac{1}{3}$ ______
21. $\frac{3}{8}$ of 62 ______
22. $\frac{5}{6} \times 47$ ______
23. $\frac{1}{5} \times 51$ ______
24. $\frac{5}{8} \times 38$ ______
25. $\frac{3}{5} \times 49$ ______
26. $\frac{2}{9} \times 25$ ______
27. $30 \times \frac{7}{8}$ ______
28. $23 \times \frac{1}{3}$ ______
29. $49 \times \frac{1}{4}$ ______
30. $62 \times \frac{7}{8}$ ______

Estimate to compare. Write > or <.

31. $\frac{1}{3} \times 16$ ◯ $\frac{1}{4} \times 15$
32. $\frac{2}{3} \times 31$ ◯ $\frac{3}{4} \times 37$
33. $\frac{2}{5} \times 24$ ◯ $\frac{5}{6} \times 19$
34. $\frac{4}{5} \times 27$ ◯ $\frac{3}{8} \times 41$
35. $\frac{7}{8} \times 47$ ◯ $\frac{5}{6} \times 59$
36. $\frac{2}{5} \times 26$ ◯ $\frac{1}{3} \times 14$
37. $\frac{7}{10} \times 35$ ◯ $\frac{1}{2} \times 41$
38. $\frac{3}{8} \times 44$ ◯ $\frac{2}{5} \times 52$
39. $\frac{4}{9}$ of 28 ◯ $\frac{1}{3} \times 59$
40. $\frac{5}{8} \times 66$ ◯ $\frac{3}{4} \times 49$
41. $\frac{1}{6} \times 47$ ◯ $\frac{1}{5} \times 33$
42. $\frac{5}{6} \times 50$ ◯ $\frac{3}{8} \times 70$

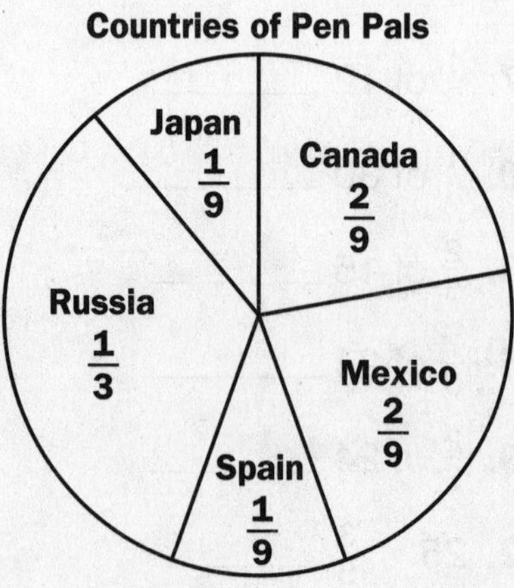

Solve. Use the circle graph above for problems 43–44.

43. When 28 students were given a choice of countries for pen pals, they chose the countries shown in the graph. About how many students chose Russia?

____

44. Of 28 students, about how many picked Canada as their choice for a pen pal?

____

Name: ______________________________

MULTIPLY FRACTIONS

Write a multiplication sentence for the models.

1. 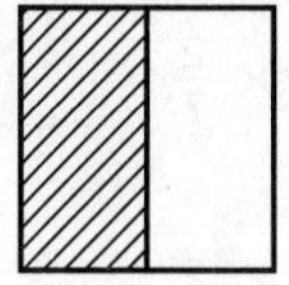

____

2. 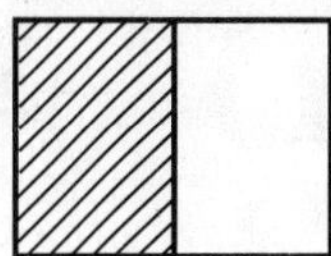 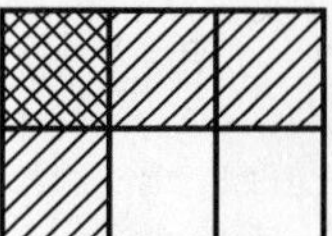

____

3. 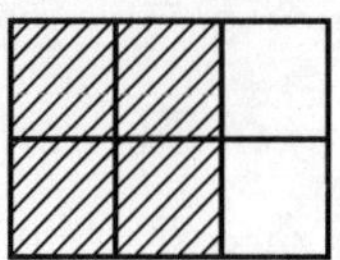 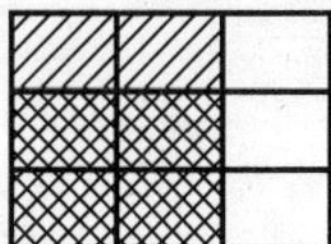

____

4. 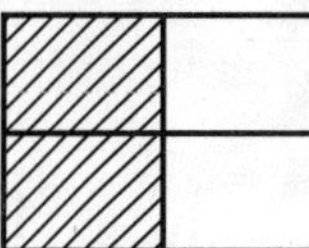 

____

5. 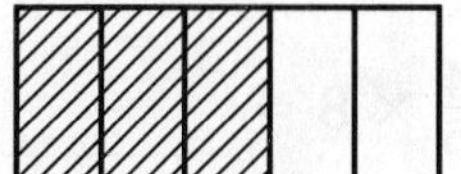 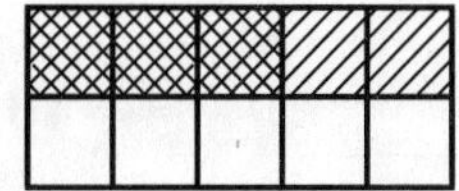

____

6. 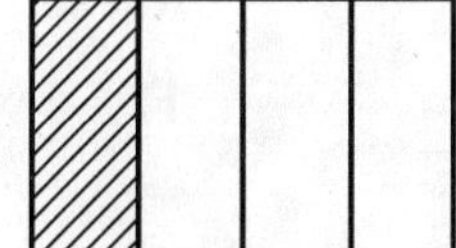 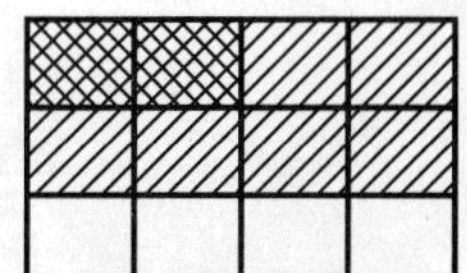

____

Multiply. You may use a model to help you.

7. $\frac{1}{3} \times \frac{3}{5} =$ ________
8. $\frac{1}{2} \times \frac{2}{3} =$ ________
9. $\frac{2}{5} \times \frac{1}{3} =$ ________
10. $\frac{2}{3} \times \frac{5}{6} =$ ________
11. $\frac{3}{4} \times \frac{1}{6} =$ ________
12. $\frac{5}{6} \times \frac{1}{2} =$ ________
13. $\frac{2}{5} \times \frac{2}{5} =$ ________
14. $\frac{1}{2} \times \frac{7}{8} =$ ________
15. $\frac{3}{10} \times \frac{1}{2} =$ ________
16. $\frac{5}{6} \times \frac{1}{3} =$ ________
17. $\frac{9}{10} \times \frac{2}{5} =$ ________
18. $\frac{9}{10} \times \frac{1}{3} =$ ________
19. $\frac{5}{12} \times \frac{2}{5} =$ ________
20. $\frac{4}{5} \times \frac{3}{4} =$ ________
21. $\frac{7}{10} \times \frac{1}{3} =$ ________
22. $\frac{3}{5} \times \frac{1}{3} =$ ________
23. $\frac{7}{8} \times \frac{1}{2} =$ ________
24. $\frac{3}{5} \times \frac{4}{5} =$ ________
25. $\frac{1}{6} \times \frac{2}{3} =$ ________
26. $\frac{5}{6} \times \frac{1}{10} =$ ________
27. $\frac{3}{10} \times \frac{1}{3} =$ ________

Practice 104

Name: ______

MULTIPLY FRACTIONS

Multiply. Write the answer in simplest form.

1. $\frac{1}{2} \times \frac{2}{3} =$ ______ **2.** $\frac{3}{7} \times \frac{1}{2} =$ ______ **3.** $\frac{1}{4} \times \frac{2}{7} =$ ______

4. $\frac{2}{5} \times \frac{2}{3} =$ ______ **5.** $\frac{1}{8} \times \frac{2}{3} =$ ______ **6.** $\frac{4}{5} \times \frac{2}{3} =$ ______

7. $\frac{3}{5} \times \frac{3}{4} =$ ______ **8.** $\frac{2}{7} \times \frac{1}{3} =$ ______ **9.** $\frac{1}{2} \times \frac{5}{9} =$ ______

10. $\frac{2}{3} \times \frac{5}{6} =$ ______ **11.** $\frac{1}{10} \times \frac{2}{5} =$ ______ **12.** $\frac{5}{6} \times \frac{2}{8} =$ ______

13. $\frac{1}{6} \times 2 =$ ______ **14.** $\frac{5}{8} \times 3 =$ ______ **15.** $7 \times \frac{1}{2} =$ ______

16. $9 \times \frac{2}{9} =$ ______ **17.** $4 \times \frac{3}{8} =$ ______ **18.** $\frac{4}{5} \times 8 =$ ______

19. $\frac{1}{2} \times \frac{1}{2} \times \frac{1}{3} =$ ______ **20.** $\frac{2}{3} \times \frac{3}{4} \times \frac{1}{2} =$ ______

21. $\frac{3}{4} \times \frac{5}{6} \times \frac{1}{3} =$ ______ **22.** $\frac{2}{5} \times \frac{1}{4} \times \frac{3}{4} =$ ______

23. What is $\frac{3}{5}$ of 30? ______ **24.** What is $\frac{3}{4}$ of 10? ______

25. What is $\frac{6}{7}$ of 28? ______ **26.** What is $\frac{1}{9}$ of $\frac{2}{3}$? ______

27. What is $\frac{9}{10}$ of $\frac{1}{3}$? ______ **28.** What is $\frac{5}{6}$ of 42? ______

Solve.

29. Kelly and her friends made a cake with $\frac{3}{4}$ cup sugar. They ate $\frac{1}{3}$ of the cake. How much sugar did they eat?

______

30. A cookie recipe uses $\frac{2}{3}$ cup flour per batch. How much flour would be needed to make 4 batches?

______

Name: ____________________

MULTIPLY MIXED NUMBERS

Multiply. Write the answer in simplest form.

1. $\frac{2}{3} \times 1\frac{1}{2} =$ ______ 2. $\frac{3}{4} \times 2\frac{1}{3} =$ ______ 3. $\frac{1}{4} \times 4\frac{1}{2} =$ ______

4. $\frac{1}{5} \times 1\frac{4}{5} =$ ______ 5. $1\frac{4}{5} \times \frac{2}{3} =$ ______ 6. $1\frac{1}{2} \times \frac{1}{4} =$ ______

7. $3\frac{1}{6} \times \frac{3}{4} =$ ______ 8. $3\frac{1}{8} \times \frac{2}{3} =$ ______ 9. $1\frac{3}{5} \times \frac{1}{3} =$ ______

10. $2\frac{5}{6} \times \frac{2}{5} =$ ______ 11. $2\frac{1}{4} \times \frac{2}{5} =$ ______ 12. $3\frac{1}{2} \times \frac{1}{2} =$ ______

13. $2 \times 1\frac{1}{2} =$ ______ 14. $1\frac{1}{3} \times 3 =$ ______ 15. $2 \times 1\frac{4}{5} =$ ______

16. $3\frac{1}{2} \times 3 =$ ______ 17. $2 \times 2\frac{1}{3} =$ ______ 18. $2 \times 2\frac{1}{6} =$ ______

Compare. Write >, <, or =.

19. $\frac{4}{5} \times 6$ ◯ $\frac{3}{4} \times 8$

20. $\frac{5}{6} \times 9$ ◯ $\frac{7}{8} \times 12$

21. $1\frac{1}{3} \times 3$ ◯ $2\frac{1}{2} \times 2$

22. $4 \times 2\frac{1}{2}$ ◯ $3\frac{1}{2} \times 2\frac{1}{2}$

23. $2\frac{1}{8} \times \frac{3}{4}$ ◯ $1\frac{7}{8} \times \frac{5}{6}$

24. $3\frac{5}{6} \times 1\frac{1}{2}$ ◯ $2\frac{1}{8} \times 3$

Solve.

25. The school cleanup crew needs $1\frac{3}{4}$ gallons of paint for each level of the building. By the end of the first day they had painted $2\frac{1}{2}$ levels. How much paint did they use during the first day?

____

26. The cleanup crew picked up paper from around the building and filled $6\frac{1}{2}$ plastic bags. If the average weight of the bags was $2\frac{1}{2}$ pounds, how many pounds of paper did they collect?

____

Name: ______________________

Problem-Solving Strategy: Solve a Simpler Problem

✔ Read
✔ Plan
✔ Solve
✔ Look Back

Solve using the solve-a-simpler-problem strategy.

1. A staircase to the top of a monument is built from stone blocks. The first 3 steps are shown below.

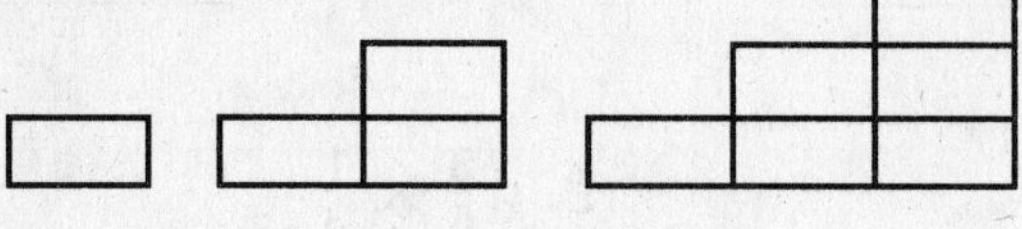

How many blocks are needed for the 10th step using this pattern?

____

2. The Hall Street Association is having a block party. There are 6 game booths labeled A, B, C, D, E, and F. The first visitor to the party lines up at game A, the second at game B, the third at game C, and so on. The seventh person gets in line at game A. In which line will the 100th visitor to the party be?

____

3. Allison, Barry, Carol, Denise, Eddie, and Frances all live along Hall Street. In how many different ways can 2 friends visit each other?

____

4. The houses on Hall Street are numbered in order from 1 to 130. How many houses have at least one 9 in their address?

____

Solve using any method.

5. Allison wants to call her friend Carol. She knows that the first five digits of Carol's phone number are 3 1 5 7 2. She remembers that the next digit is either 8 or 9, but cannot remember the last digit. How many different possibilities are there for Carol's phone number?

____

6. Barry, Denise, Eddie, and Frances live at the following addresses on Hall Street: 17, 23, 79, and 115, but not in that order. Use the clues to match each person with their address.
   - Denise lives at an address that is not a prime number.
   - The sum of the digits of Barry's address is twice the sum of Eddie's.

____

Name: ____________________

Divide Fractions

Write a division sentence for the models.

1.

$\frac{1}{3}$	$\frac{1}{3}$	$\frac{1}{3}$

$\frac{1}{3}$	$\frac{1}{3}$	$\frac{1}{3}$

____

2.

$\frac{1}{4}$	$\frac{1}{4}$	$\frac{1}{4}$	$\frac{1}{4}$

$\frac{1}{4}$	$\frac{1}{4}$	$\frac{1}{4}$	$\frac{1}{4}$

$\frac{1}{4}$	$\frac{1}{4}$	$\frac{1}{4}$	$\frac{1}{4}$

$\frac{1}{4}$	$\frac{1}{4}$	$\frac{1}{4}$	$\frac{1}{4}$

____

3.

$\frac{1}{5}$	$\frac{1}{5}$	$\frac{1}{5}$	$\frac{1}{5}$	$\frac{1}{5}$

$\frac{1}{5}$	$\frac{1}{5}$	$\frac{1}{5}$	$\frac{1}{5}$	$\frac{1}{5}$

____

4.

$\frac{1}{8}$	$\frac{1}{8}$	$\frac{1}{8}$	$\frac{1}{8}$	$\frac{1}{8}$	$\frac{1}{8}$

$\frac{2}{8}$ $\frac{2}{8}$ $\frac{2}{8}$

____

5.

$\frac{1}{10}$	$\frac{1}{10}$	$\frac{1}{10}$	$\frac{1}{10}$	$\frac{1}{10}$	$\frac{1}{10}$

$\frac{3}{10}$ $\frac{3}{10}$

____

6.

$\frac{1}{5}$	$\frac{1}{5}$	$\frac{1}{5}$	$\frac{1}{5}$

$\frac{2}{5}$ $\frac{2}{5}$

____

Divide. Use fraction strips if you want.

7. $2 \div \frac{1}{7} =$ ______ 8. $3 \div \frac{1}{5} =$ ______ 9. $4 \div \frac{1}{4} =$ ______

10. $5 \div \frac{1}{2} =$ ______ 11. $6 \div \frac{1}{3} =$ ______ 12. $4 \div \frac{1}{5} =$ ______

13. $\frac{3}{4} \div \frac{1}{4} =$ ______ 14. $\frac{5}{6} \div \frac{1}{6} =$ ______ 15. $\frac{10}{12} \div \frac{5}{12} =$ ______

16. $\frac{7}{8} \div \frac{1}{8} =$ ______ 17. $\frac{6}{10} \div \frac{3}{10} =$ ______ 18. $\frac{4}{8} \div \frac{2}{8} =$ ______

19. $\frac{8}{10} \div \frac{2}{10} =$ ______ 20. $\frac{6}{9} \div \frac{3}{9} =$ ______ 21. $\frac{8}{10} \div \frac{2}{10} =$ ______

22. $\frac{6}{12} \div \frac{3}{12} =$ ______ 23. $\frac{2}{6} \div \frac{1}{6} =$ ______ 24. $\frac{6}{8} \div \frac{3}{8} =$ ______

25. $\frac{3}{12} \div \frac{1}{12} =$ ______ 26. $\frac{4}{8} \div \frac{4}{8} =$ ______ 27. $\frac{4}{6} \div \frac{2}{6} =$ ______

28. $\frac{9}{10} \div \frac{9}{10} =$ ______ 29. $\frac{10}{12} \div \frac{5}{12} =$ ______ 30. $\frac{3}{5} \div \frac{1}{5} =$ ______

Name: ______________________

Problem Solving: Choose Whether to Use Fractions or Decimals

✔ Read
✔ Plan
✔ Solve
✔ Look Back

Solve. Use the menu to answer problems 1–5.

PIZZA	
Whole Pie or by the Slice	
Large Pie (8 slices)	$13.00
Slice	$1.75
Small Pie (6 slices)	$10.50

1. Ten friends visit the restaurant for lunch. Each of them has $3.50. What should they order so that they get the greatest number of slices? How much money will they have left after ordering?

____

____

2. The restaurant charges by the slice for up to 3 slices. For 4 large slices they charge one half the price of a large pie. How much more do you pay for $1\frac{1}{2}$ large pies than for 1 large pie and 3 slices?

____

3. If you were planning a pizza party and needed at least 20 slices of any size, what would you order to spend the least amount of money? (You can order half pies if you like.) How much would you have to spend?

____

4. How much more would you pay for $3\frac{1}{2}$ small pies than for $2\frac{1}{2}$ large pies?

____

5. After the first few customers have eaten lunch, the restaurant has taken in $26.25. What did the first few customers order?

____

Solve using any method.

6. Lana, Maria, Ned, Oscar, and Pamela are sitting at a round table at the restaurant. Lana is between Maria and Ned. Maria is between Lana and Oscar. Between which two friends is Pamela sitting?

____

7. Jane, Will, Pete, Oscar, and Ned are waiting in line at the movie theater. Jane is first in line and Oscar is behind Pete. Ned is last and behind Oscar. Where is Will standing?

____

Name: ____________________

PERIMETER AND AREA

Find the perimeter and area.

1. 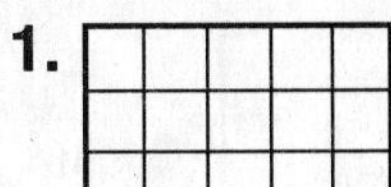

Perimeter: ________

Area: ________

2.

Perimeter: ________

Area: ________

3.

Perimeter: ________

Area: ________

4. 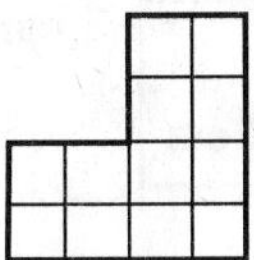

Perimeter: ________

Area: ________

5. 

Perimeter: ________

Area: ________

6. 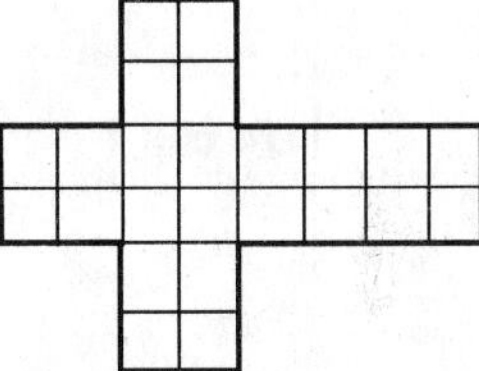

Perimeter: ________

Area: ________

Find the perimeter.

7. 16 cm, 25 cm

____

8. 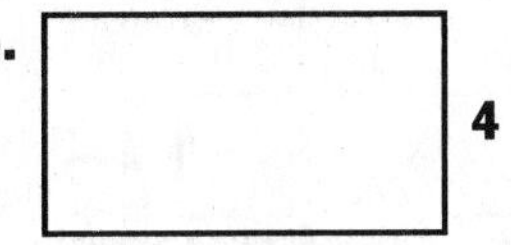

4 cm, 6.5 cm

____

9. 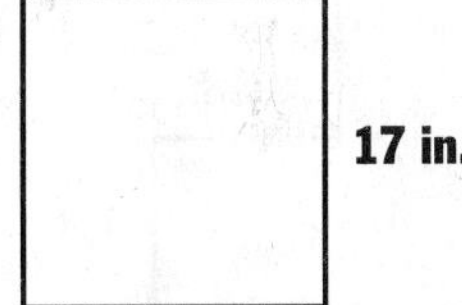

17 in.

____

10. rectangle
$l = 14$ cm
$w = 11$ cm

____

11. rectangle
$l = 75$ cm
$w = 50$ cm

____

12. rectangle
$l = 4\frac{1}{2}$ in.
$w = 3\frac{1}{2}$ in.

____

13. square
$l = 9$ m
$w = 9$ m

____

Solve.

14. A square has a perimeter of 36 units. What is the area of the square?

____

15. A square has an area of 64 square units. What is its perimeter?

____

Name: ____________________ Practice 110

AREA OF RECTANGLES

Find the area.

1. 3 in. 12 in.

____

2. 12 cm 30 cm

____

3. 9 mm 16 mm

____

4. 14 cm 14 cm

____

5.

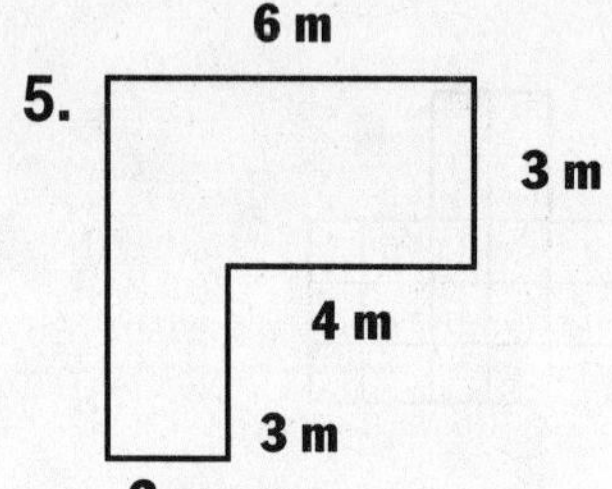

____

6.

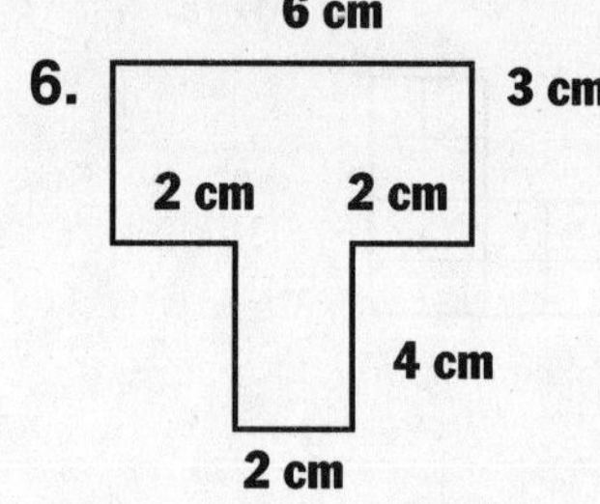

____

7. 3 ft 3 ft 3 ft 3 ft

____

8.

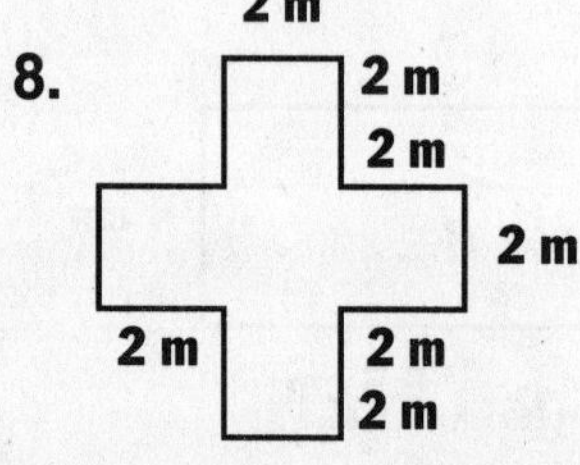

____

9.

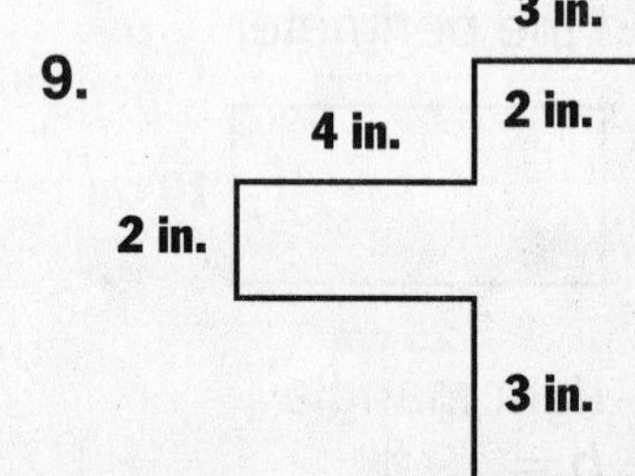

____

Solve. Use the table to answer problems 10–11.

10. What is the area of the football field?

____

11. Which sport has a field with an area of exactly 8,800 square yards?

____

Sport	Dimensions of field
Football	100 yd long, 53 yd wide
Field hockey	100 yd long, 60 yd wide
Soccer	110 yd long, 80 yd wide
Rugby	160 yd long, 75 yd wide

Name: ______________________

AREA OF RIGHT TRIANGLES

Find the area.

1. 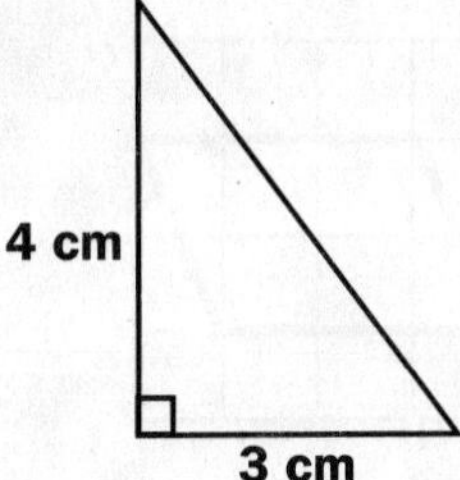

2. 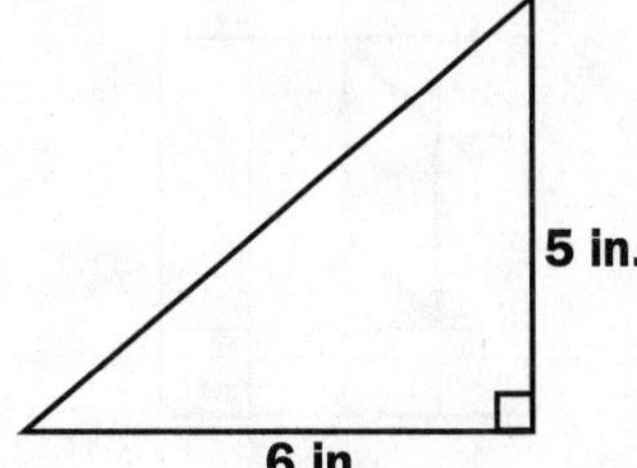

3. 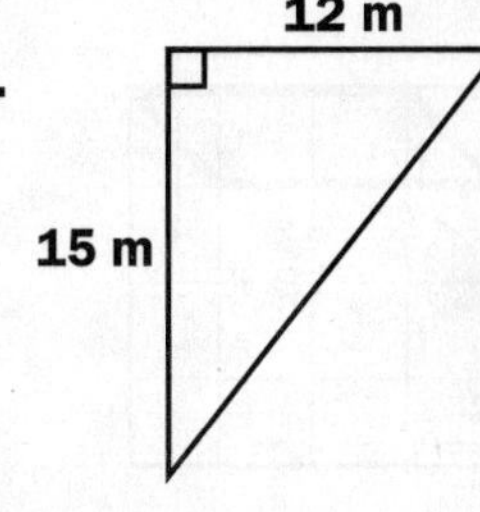

4. 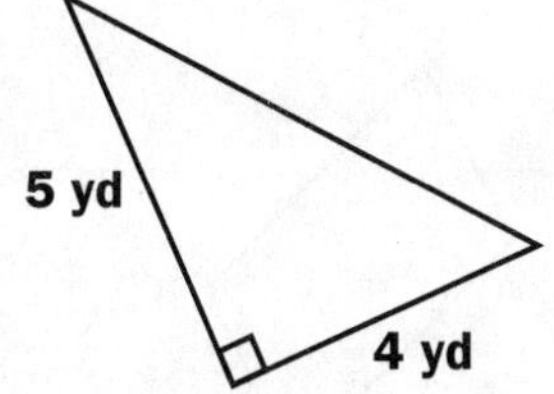

5. 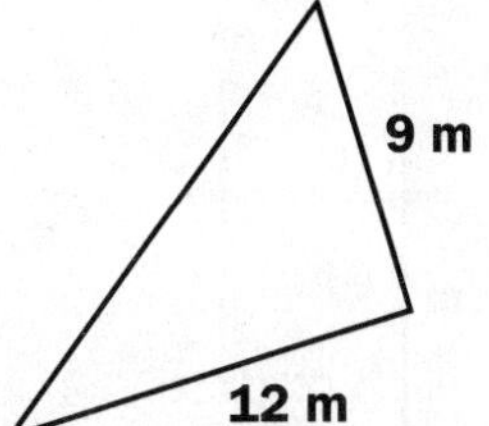

6. 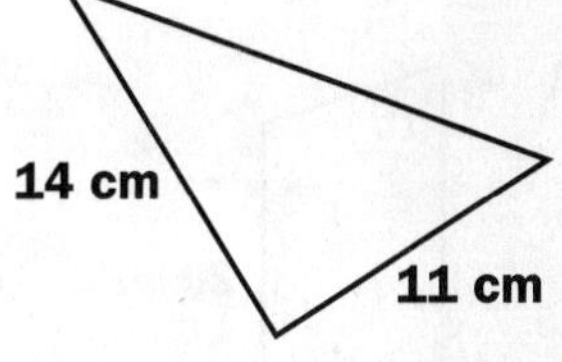

7. right triangle
$b = 12$ m
$h = 20$ m

8. right triangle
$b = 18$ in.
$h = 3$ in.

9. right triangle
$b = 16$ cm
$h = 9$ cm

10. right triangle
$b = 19$ ft
$h = 2.6$ ft

11. right triangle
$b = \frac{1}{2}$ in.
$h = 2$ in.

12. right triangle
$b = 7.5$ m
$h = 4$ m

Solve.

13. Which has a greater area, a triangle with a base of 8 m and a height of 6 m, or a triangle with a base of 5 m and a height of 8 m?

14. A rectangle has a length of 16 cm and a width of 10 cm. It is cut in half to make two right triangles. What is the area of one of the triangles?

Name: ______________________

Area of Parallelograms

Find the area.

1. 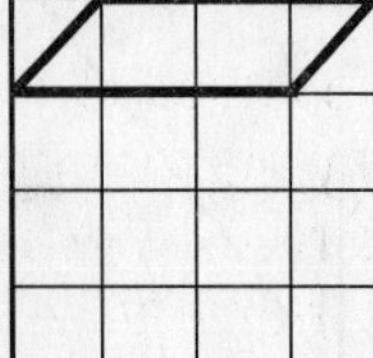

____

2. 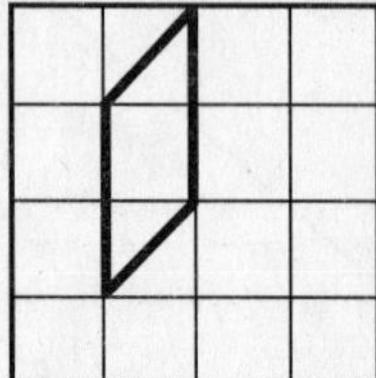

____

3. 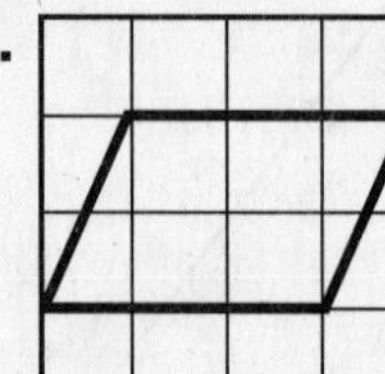

____

4. 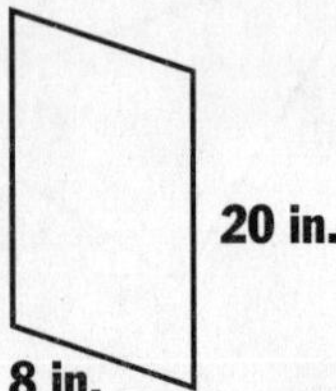

____

5. 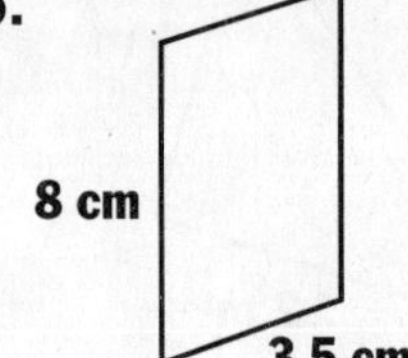

____

6. 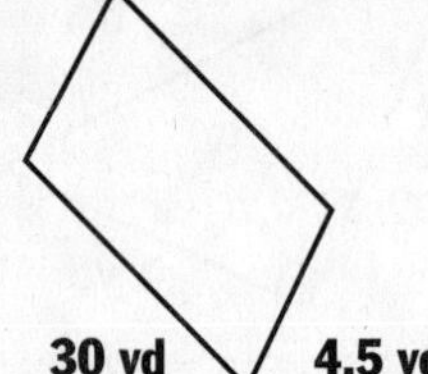

____

7. parallelogram
base = 8 m
height = 21 m

____

8. parallelogram
base = 4.5 cm
height = 3.1 cm

____

9. parallelogram
base = $5\frac{1}{2}$ m
height = 3 m

____

Find the base and height of the figure. Then find the area. Let 1 grid square equal 1 square unit.

10. 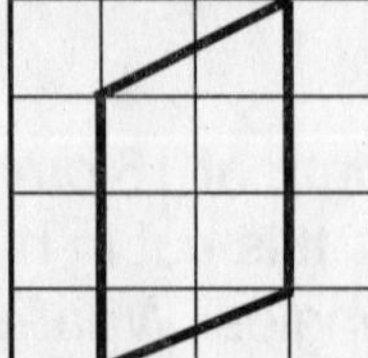

____

____

11. 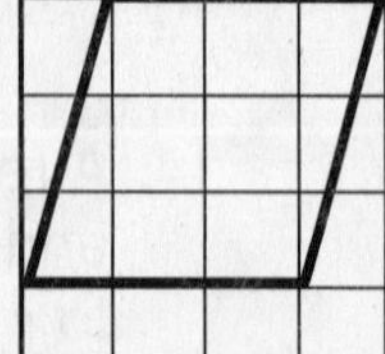

____

____

12. 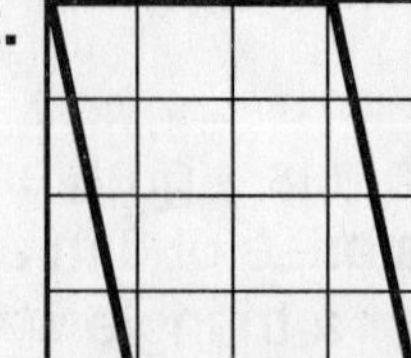

____

____

Name: ____________________

Problem-Solving Strategy: Make a Model

✔ Read
✔ Plan
✔ Solve
✔ Look Back

Solve using the make-a-model strategy.

1. For her birthday party, Connie's parents will rent square tables. Each table can seat one person on a side. In how many different ways can 3 of the tables be arranged to seat exactly 8 people? Make a sketch.

   ____

2. Connie wants all the tables to be touching so that they make one large table. If her parents rent 5 tables, what is the greatest number of people that can be seated?

   ____

3. There will be 18 people altogether at the party. What is the least number of tables Connie's parents must rent if they are to be put together to form one large table?

   ____

4. Two friends call to say that they cannot attend the party. Connie arranges the 8 square tables to seat exactly 16 people. Show an arrangement she can use.

Solve using any method.

5. Connie's circular birthday cake has 1 candle more than her age and a small flower between every two candles. Connie is 11 years old. How many flowers are on the cake?

   ____

6. For dessert, there is a choice of birthday cake, ice cream, fruit salad, apple pie, and cookies. How many different combinations of 2 desserts can be made?

   ____

Name: ________________________________

Practice 114

Circumference

Find the circumference. Use 3.14 for π.

1. 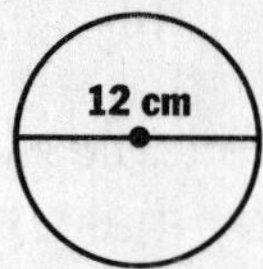

2. 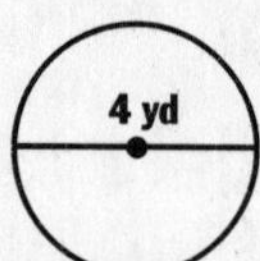

3. 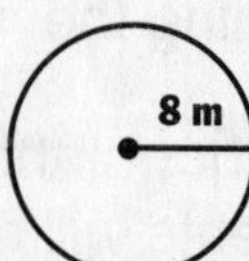

4. 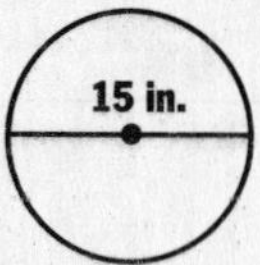

5. 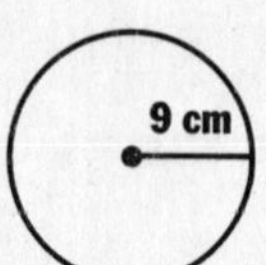

6. 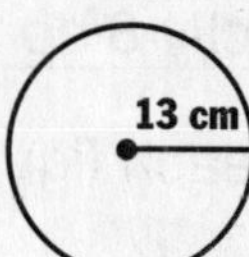

7. 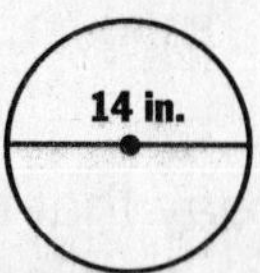

8. 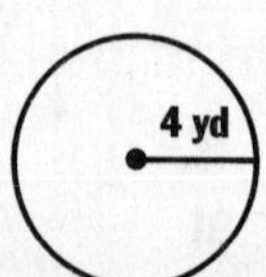

9. 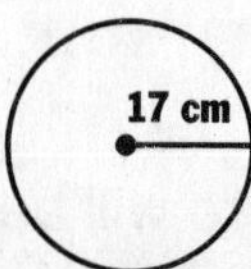

10. circle
diameter = 9 mm

11. circle
diameter = 11 m

12. circle
diameter = 35 in.

13. circle
radius = 3 mm

14. circle
radius = 10 in.

15. circle
radius = 35 cm

Solve.

16. A circular pool has a diameter of about 32 feet. What is the approximate distance around the rim of the pool?

17. Donna is marking off a play area using a string that is 15 feet long. A friend is holding one end of the string while Donna holds the other end and walks around in a circle. About how many feet will Donna walk to complete the circle?

Name:

3-DIMENSIONAL FIGURES

Name each 3-dimensional figure.

1. 

2. 

3. 

4. 

Name each figure and write the number of faces, edges, and vertices.

5. 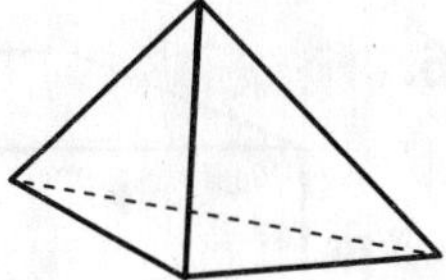

6. 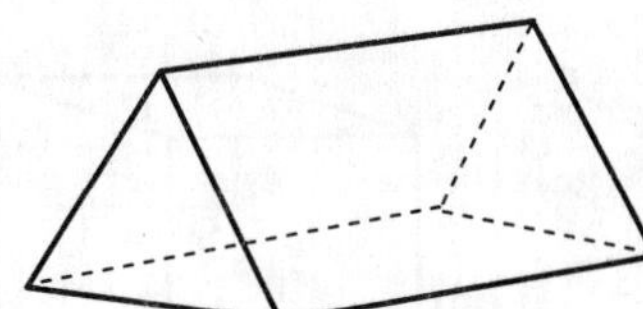

7. 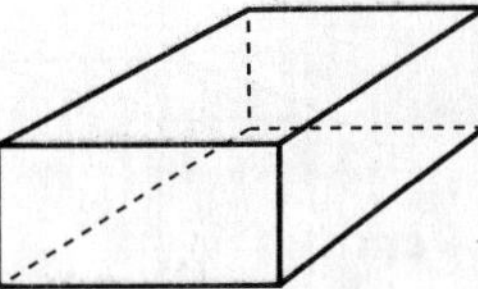

8. 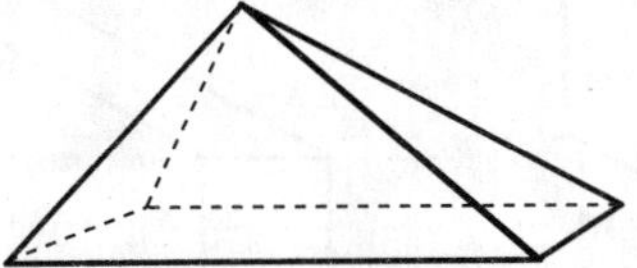

9. 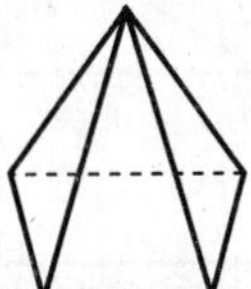

10. 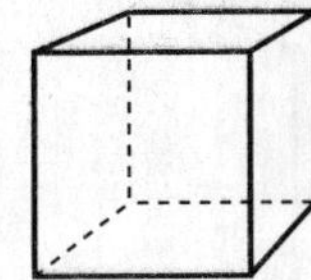

11. 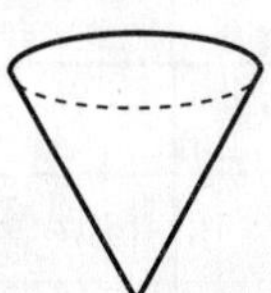

12. 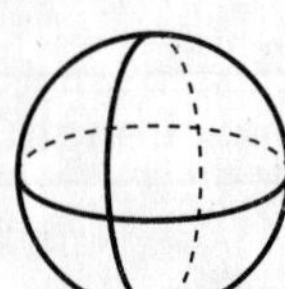

13. 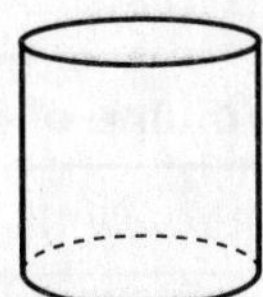

Name:

VOLUME

Find the volume.

1.

2.

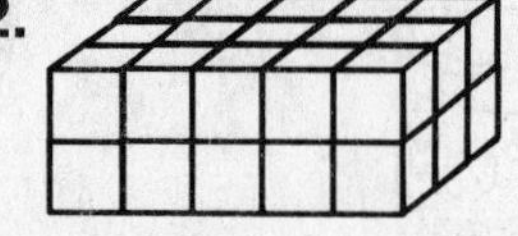

3.

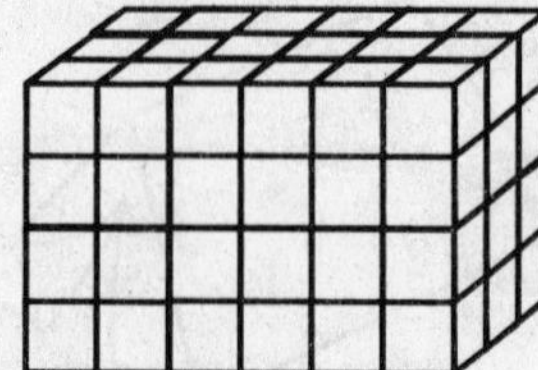

4.

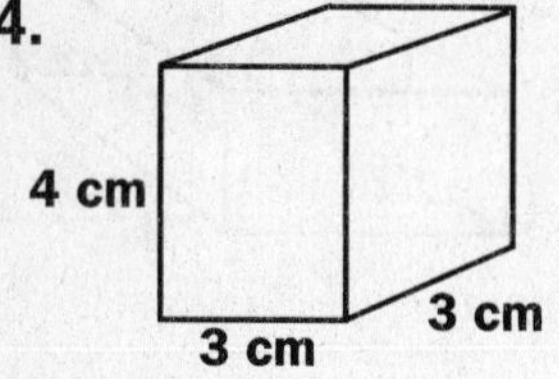

5.

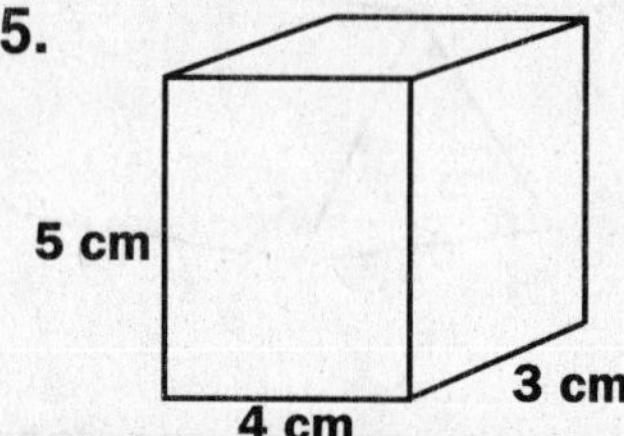

6.

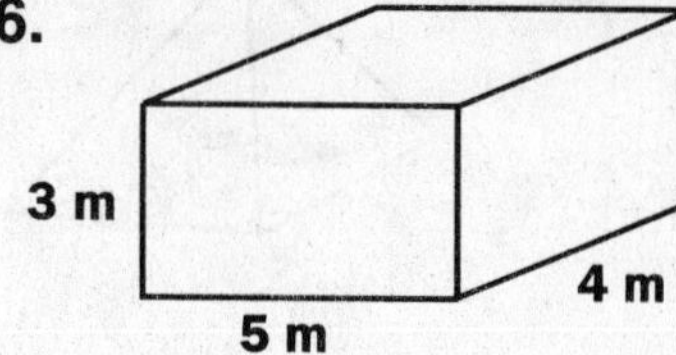

7.

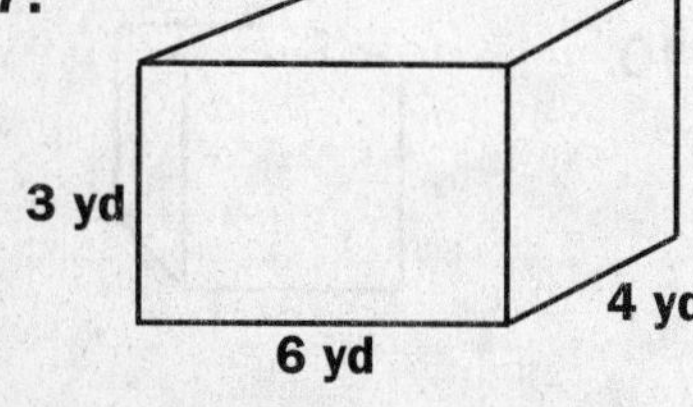

8.

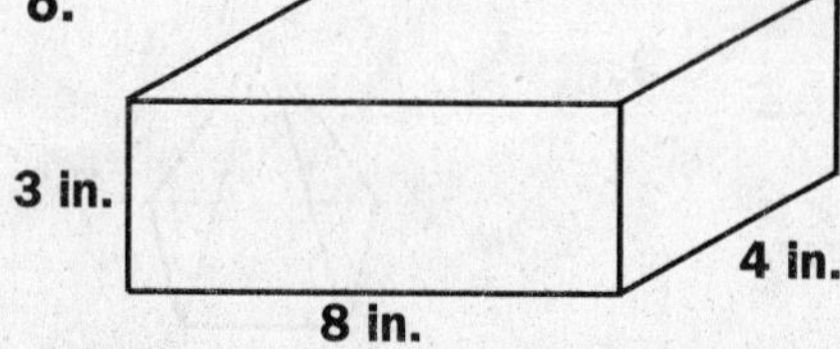

9.

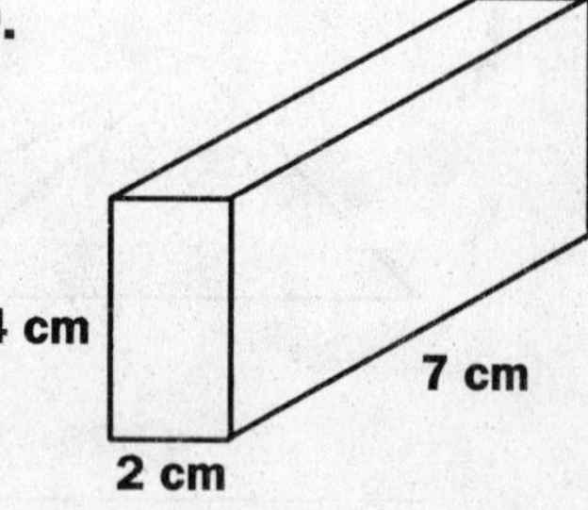

Complete the table.

	Volume of Rectangular Prism	Length	Width	Height
10.	40 in.^{3}		2 in.	4 in.
11.	144 yd^3	6 yd		6 yd
12.	72 cm^3	4 cm	6 cm	
13.	360 m^3	0.6 m		60 m

Name: ______________________

Problem Solving: Solve Multistep Problems

✔ Read
✔ Plan
✔ Solve
✔ Look Back

Solve each multistep problem.

1. Rachel is arranging her new bedroom. The floor is a square with a perimeter of 64 ft. What is the area of the room? What is the remaining area available on the floor after a 6 ft by 3 ft bed is placed in the room?

   ____

2. Rachel buys a bookshelf that she can assemble on her own. She can decide how high to build it. The volume of her room is 2,560 cubic ft, and its floor perimeter is 64 ft. What can be the maximum height of the bookshelf, from floor to ceiling?

   ____

3. Rachel assembles a bookshelf with four shelves. Each shelf has a volume of 10 cubic ft, a height of 1 ft, and a width of 2 ft. What are the dimensions of the whole bookshelf?

   ____

   ____

   ____

4. The window in Rachel's room has a special shape. It is made up of a 4 ft wide by 3 ft high rectangle with a half-circle on top. The circle's diameter lies along the width of the rectangle. What is the total perimeter of the window? (Hint: Find half a circle's circumference + part of a rectangle's perimeter.)

   ____

   ____

Solve using any method.

5. Caroline gets an allowance for doing chores around the house. Each week she gets \$0.75 each for the first 5 chores and \$1.25 for each additional chore. Last week she earned \$8.75. How many household chores did Caroline do?

   ____

   ____

6. Caroline keeps a calendar to check off the number of days until her birthday. On June 29, she counted 71 more days. If school begins on Monday, September 1, on what day of the week is Caroline's birthday this year? Explain.

   ____

   ____

RATIOS

Practice 118

Name: ______________________________

Use the shapes to find the ratio. Write the ratio in three ways.

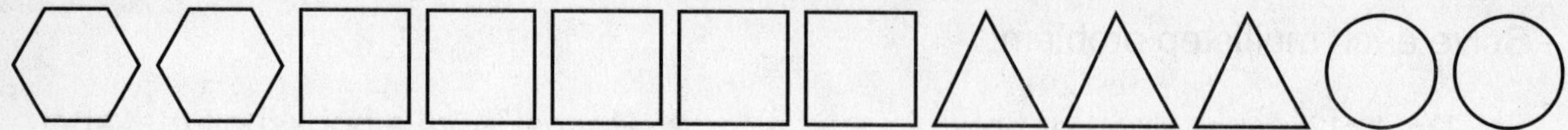

1. squares to triangles ______________

2. hexagons to circles ______________

3. circles to squares ______________

4. triangles to squares ______________

5. squares to hexagons ______________

6. total shapes to hexagons ______________

7. total shapes to squares ______________

8. circles to total shapes ______________

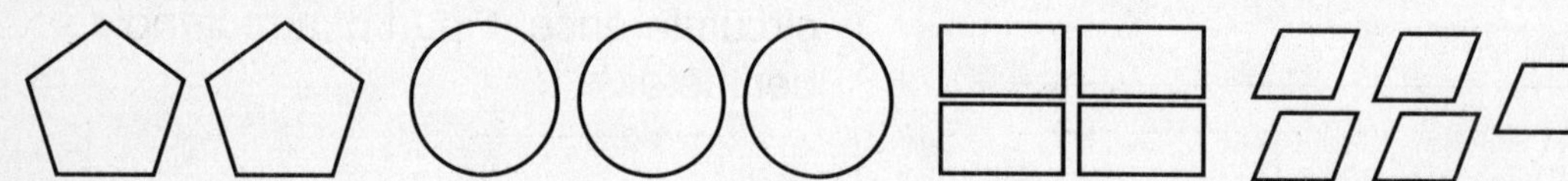

9. circles to rectangles ______________

10. squares to rhombuses ______________

11. rectangles to pentagons ______________

12. rhombuses to rectangles ______________

Write or draw a situation to represent the ratio.

13. 1 to 10 ______________

14. 4:1 ______________

15. $\frac{24}{1}$ ______________

16. 1 to 12 ______________

Name:

Equal Ratios

Complete the ratio table.

1.

1	2	3	4	5
8	16			40

2.

1		3	4	
4	8			20

3.

1	2		4	
6		18		30

4.

3	6	9	12	
4	8			20

5.

3	6		12	15
8		24		

6.

8		24	32	
5	10			25

Use counters or a ratio table to find the equal ratios.

7. $\frac{1}{7} = \frac{\square}{14} = \frac{\square}{21} = \frac{\square}{28}$

8. $\frac{3}{6} = \frac{\square}{12} = \frac{\square}{18} = \frac{\square}{24}$

9. $\frac{2}{3} = \frac{\square}{6} = \frac{\square}{9} = \frac{\square}{12}$

10. $\frac{5}{1} = \frac{\square}{2} = \frac{\square}{3} = \frac{\square}{4}$

11. $\frac{3}{5} = \frac{\square}{10} = \frac{\square}{15} = \frac{\square}{20}$

12. $\frac{3}{2} = \frac{\square}{4} = \frac{\square}{6} = \frac{\square}{8}$

13. $\frac{2}{7} = \frac{4}{\square} = \frac{6}{\square} = \frac{8}{\square}$

14. $\frac{5}{4} = \frac{10}{\square} = \frac{15}{\square} = \frac{20}{\square}$

Solve. For each picture, draw another picture to show an equal ratio.

15. □□□
○○○○

16. △△
□□□□□

Name: ______________________________

FIND EQUAL RATIOS

Are the ratios equal? Write *yes* or *no*.

1. $\frac{3}{5}, \frac{9}{15}$ ____________

2. $\frac{4}{9}, \frac{8}{20}$ ____________

3. $\frac{5}{8}, \frac{15}{32}$ ____________

4. $\frac{3}{2}, \frac{12}{8}$ ____________

5. $\frac{18}{6}, \frac{1}{3}$ ____________

6. $\frac{14}{7}, \frac{2}{1}$ ____________

7. $\frac{25}{10}, \frac{5}{2}$ ____________

8. $\frac{6}{7}, \frac{12}{14}$ ____________

9. $\frac{1}{3}, \frac{5}{15}$ ____________

10. $\frac{3}{4}, \frac{5}{6}$ ____________

11. $\frac{9}{10}, \frac{18}{21}$ ____________

12. $\frac{12}{4}, \frac{3}{1}$ ____________

13. 8:3, 16:6 ____________

14. 21:14, 2:3 ____________

15. 3:5, 12:20 ____________

16. 4:10, 8:15 ____________

17. 15:3, 1:5 ____________

18. 6:7, 18:21 ____________

19. 9:3, 3:1 ____________

20. 1:2, 9:18 ____________

21. 7:15, 14:21 ____________

22. 8:10, 24:30 ____________

23. 6:9, 18:27 ____________

24. 24:32, 9:16 ____________

Algebra Complete to make equal ratios.

25. $2:3 = \frac{\square}{15}$

26. $9:7 = 18:\square$

27. $6:8 = \frac{\square}{4}$

28. $1:4 = 3:\square$

Solve.

29. A teacher uses 3 packages of paper every 5 weeks. At this rate, how long will 12 packages of paper last?

____

30. The children use 3 jars of paint for every 2 posters they make. How many jars of paint will they need to make 12 posters?

____

Name: ____________________

SCALE DRAWINGS

Use a metric ruler, the scale, and the scale drawing to find the actual dimensions of the ship.

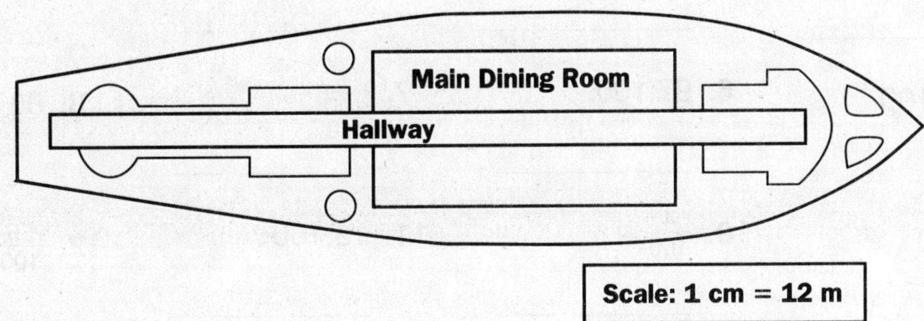

Scale: 1 cm = 12 m

1. Length of the main dining room: 4 cm

Actual length ____________

2. Length of the longest hallway: 10 cm

Actual length ____________

3. Width of the ship at the widest part: 3 cm

Actual width ____________

4. Total length of the ship: 12 cm

Actual length ____________

Use a metric ruler and the scale drawing to find the actual dimensions of each room.

Scale: 1 cm = 2 m

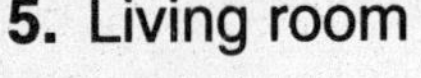

5. Living room ____________

6. Den ____________

7. Dining room ____________

8. Kitchen ____________

9. Bathroom ____________

10. Garage ____________

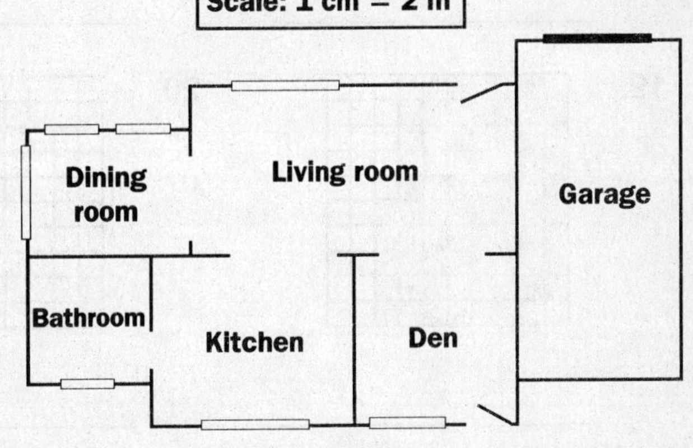

Name: ______________________________

MEANING OF PERCENT

Write the ratio as a percent.

1. $\frac{21}{100}$ ________
2. 32:100 ________
3. 16 to 100 ________
4. $\frac{3}{100}$ ________
5. 45 to 100 ________
6. 97:100 ________
7. $\frac{1}{100}$ ________
8. 88 to 100 ________
9. 50:100 ________
10. $\frac{4}{100}$ ________
11. 19:100 ________
12. $\frac{56}{100}$ ________

What percent of the grid is shaded? unshaded?

13. 
____

14. 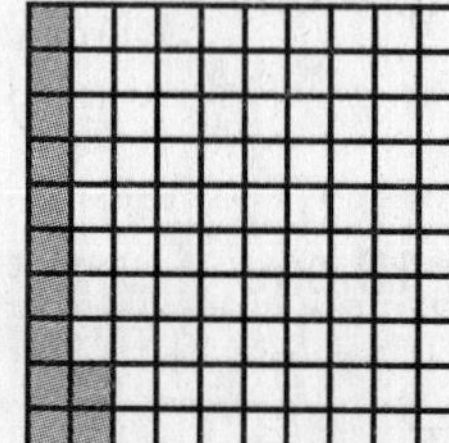
____

15. 
____

16. 
____

17. 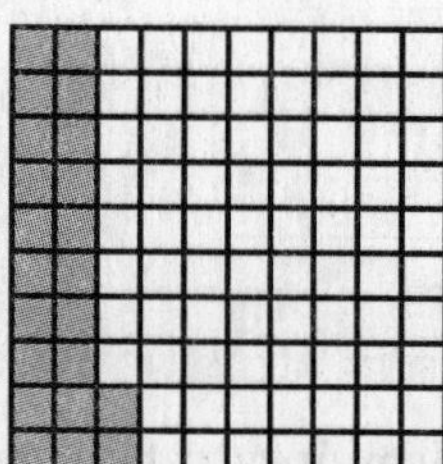
____

18. 
____

19. 
____

20. 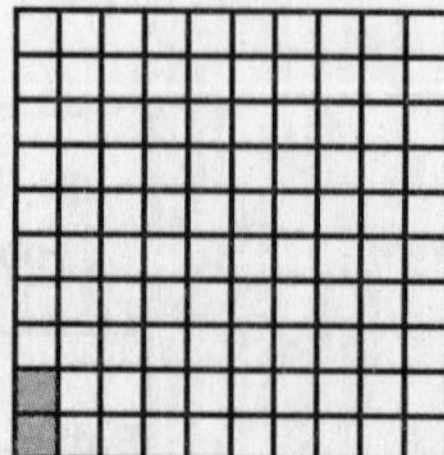
____

21. 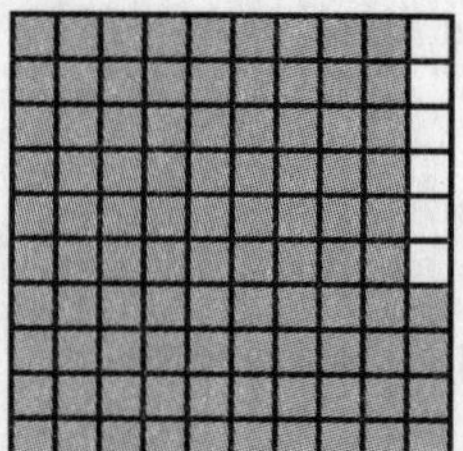
____

Practice 123

Name: ____________________

RELATE PERCENTS, FRACTIONS, AND DECIMALS

Write as a percent, a fraction in simplest form, and a decimal.

1. 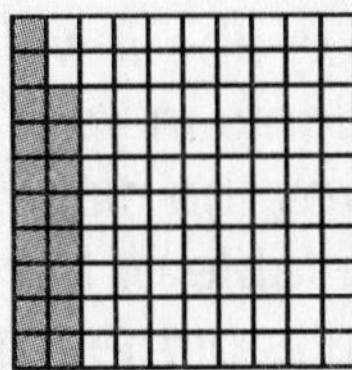
____

2. 
____

3. 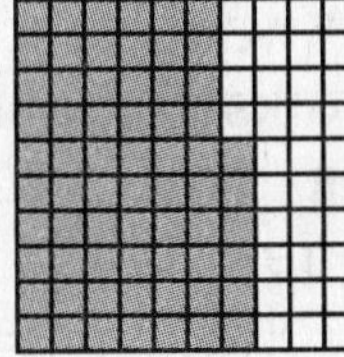
____

4. 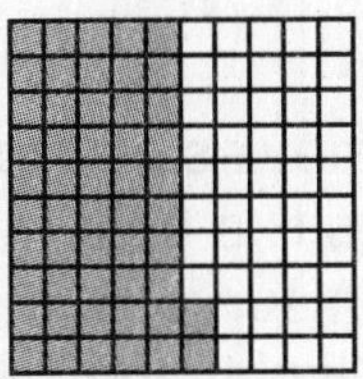
____

5. 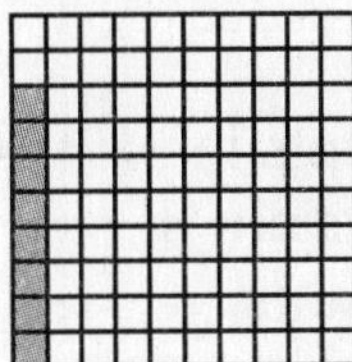
____

6. 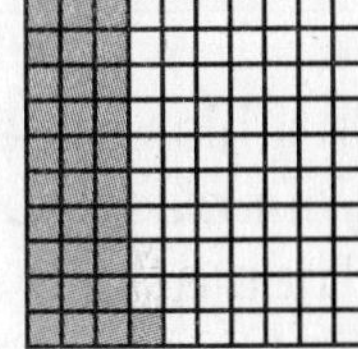
____

7. 14 percent ____________

8. 70 out of 100 ____________

9. 49 hundredths ____________

10. 13 out of 100 ____________

11. 90 percent ____________

12. 56 out of 100 ____________

Complete the table. Write fractions in simplest form.

13.

Percent	Decimal	Fraction
15%		
25%		
40%		
65%		
90%		

14.

Percent	Decimal	Fraction
6%		
11%		
36%		
62%		
84%		

Name: ______________________

Practice 124

Problem-Solving Strategy: Conduct an Experiment

✔ Read
✔ Plan
✔ Solve
✔ Look Back

Solve using the conduct-an-experiment strategy.

1. A waiter drops a tray containing 20 forks. Do more forks land right side up, upside down, or on their side? Predict what you think will happen. Conduct an experiment by dropping a fork 20 times. Use a table to record and display your results.

____

2. Make a prediction about which months the students in your class were born. Survey the class. Display your results in a table or bar graph. How do the results of the experiment compare to your prediction?

____

3. In which state were most students in your class born? Make a prediction. Then ask 20 students to name the state in which they were born. Record the results in a table.

____

4. What kinds of movies do most of your classmates like best? Make a prediction. Then survey the students in your class. Display the results in a table or bar graph.

____

Solve using any method.

5. For her birthday, Jamie invited 5 friends to a party. The first one to arrive brought 1 guest. The second friend had 3 guests. Each of the next 3 friends had 2 more guests than the one before. How many people were at Jamie's party?

____

6. Sam, Sara, Stacy, and Steve rode go-carts at the state fair. They picked cars numbered 7, 9, 15, and 20. Steve rode a car with a prime number. Steve's sister had the only even-numbered car. Sara had the car whose number had only 3 factors. Which numbered car did each person ride?

____

____

7. Mr. Cody wanted to drive 5 students to a concert. However, his car could only hold 3 of them. How many different combinations of 3 students could he drive?

____

Name:

PROBABILITY

Use the spinner for problems 1–4.

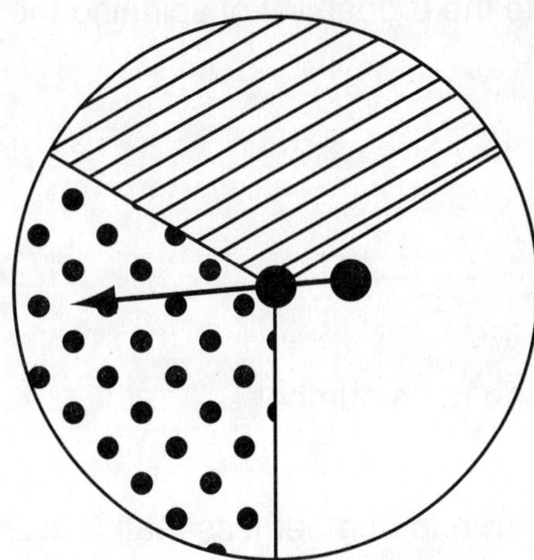

1. How many possible outcomes are there when you spin the spinner? What are they?

2. Is each outcome equally likely, more likely, or less likely? Why?

3. Use a spinner like the one shown and spin it 30 times. Record the results in a frequency table.

4. Did the results of your experiment in problem 3 match your answer to problem 2?

Use the bag with the cubes for problems 5–8.

5. How many possible outcomes are there if you pick a cube out of the bag with your eyes closed? What are they?

6. Which outcome is most likely? Why?

7. Which outcome is least likely?

8. What cubes would you add to the bag to make all the outcomes equally likely?

Practice 126

Name: ______________________________

PROBABILITY

Use the spinner for exercises 1–7.
Write the probability of spinning the number.

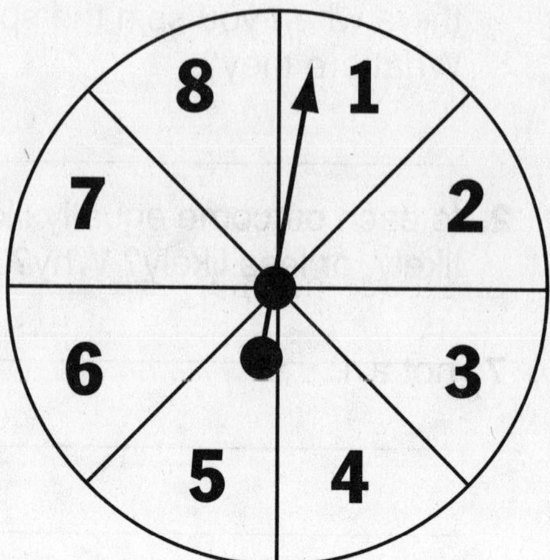

1. 8 ______ **2.** 5 ______

3. 1 ______ **4.** 0 ______

5. an even number ______________

6. an odd number less than 6 ______________

7. an even number less than 5 ______________

Suppose you write the names of the 12 months on cards.
You then pick a card without looking. Find the probability.

8. a month that begins with the letter J ______________

9. a month that is spelled with 5 letters ______________

10. a month that is spelled with fewer than 6 letters ______________

Solve.

11. You and 3 friends are trying to decide which one of you will be the president of a new club. If you put each name on a card and pick one without looking, what is the probability that your name will be chosen?

____

12. There are 5 suggestions for the name of the club. If you put each name on a card and pick one without looking, what is the probability of picking the one that is your favorite?

____

Name: ___

PREDICT OUTCOMES

Predict how many times you will spin the number in 40 spins.

1. an even number ___
2. a prime number ___
3. 2 ___
4. 3 ___
5. an odd number ___
6. 5 ___
7. not a 1 ___
8. not a prime number ___
9. not a 3 ___
10. not a 2 ___

The books on the shelf are all identical in size and shape. Predict how many times you will choose the book named in 50 tries without looking. Assume that you return the book to the shelf after each choice.

11. math book ___
12. dictionary ___
13. Spanish book ___
14. not a Spanish book ___
15. not a science book ___
16. a book ___
17. not a math book ___
18. not a dictionary ___
19. science book ___
20. English book ___

Complete the experiment.

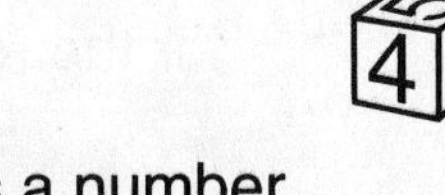

21. Predict how many times a number cube will land on 5 in 30 rolls. Roll a number cube 30 times. How does your prediction compare to the actual results?

___

___

___

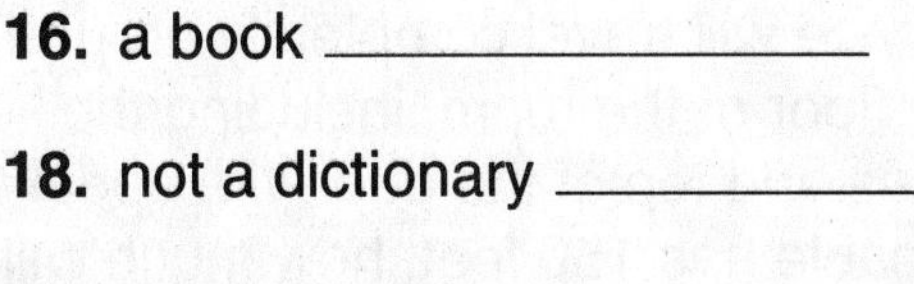

22. If you repeat problem 21 using 300 rolls of the number cube, how do you think the results will compare to your previous results?

___

___

___

___

Name: Practice 128

PROBLEM SOLVING: USE DATA FROM A DRAWING

✔ Read
✔ Plan
✔ Solve
✔ Look Back

Solve using the use-data-from-a-drawing strategy.

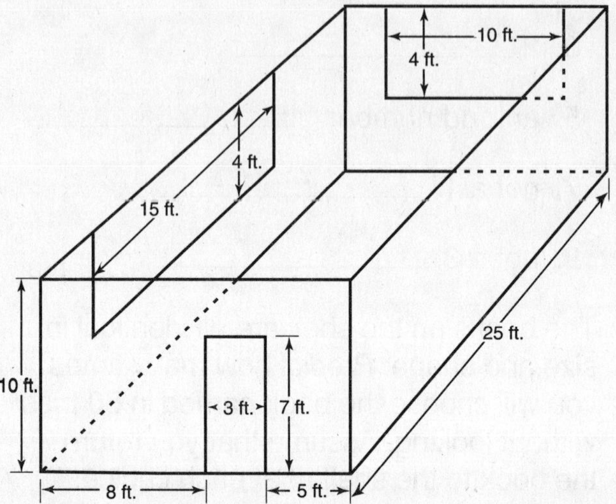

1. The room shown in the drawing is being remodeled. The entire floor will be covered with 1-foot square tiles. The tiles are sold in boxes of 12. What is the least number of boxes the homeowners will have to buy?

2. Each of the walls that has a window is going to be painted. A quart of paint covers 100 square feet and costs $4.49. The same paint costs $15.99 a gallon. About how much money should be budgeted for paint for the 2 walls?

3. Wiring for cable and telephone service will travel completely around the floor of the room, including the sides and top of the door. If a spool of cable has 150 feet, how much will be left after the room is wired?

4. An appliance store salesperson says that if the volume of the room is between 3,500 and 4,500 cubic feet, an air conditioner will cost $565. If the volume is greater than 4,500 cubic feet, the correct air conditioner will be $719. Which model is needed for the room shown?

Solve using any method.

5. Steven has a bag of 32 crayons and markers. There are 5 crayons for every 3 markers. How many crayons and markers does Steven have?

6. When Judith walks 3 more blocks, she will be halfway to school. If she has already walked 2 blocks, how far does she live from school?